NASTY
Women

J

Chica *City*

M

The McGraw·Hill Companies

Library of Congress Cataloging-in-Publication Data

Carter, Jay.
    Nasty women / Jay Carter.
        p.   cm.
    Includes bibliographical references (p. 117).
    ISBN 0-07-141023-6
      1. Control (Psychology).   2. Women—Psychology.   3. Abusive women.
  4. Interpersonal relations.   I. Title.

    BF632.5 .C365   2003
    155.3'33—dc21   2003046055

1 2 3 4 5 6 7 8 9 0   AGM/AGM   2 1 0 9 8 7 6 5 4 3

ISBN 0-07-141023-6

Interior design by Nick Panos

McGraw-Hill books are available at special quantity discounts to use as premiums and sales promotions, or for use in corporate training programs. For more information, please write to the Director of Special Sales, Professional Publishing, McGraw-Hill, Two Penn Plaza, New York, NY 10121-2298. Or contact your local bookstore.

This book is printed on acid-free paper.

Contents

Acknowledgments

Many thanks to the following people for their help with the book: Lotes Gudez, Dr. Michelle Munson, Sheila Sen-Carter, Darin Acopan, Kim Riggs, Maxine Goodwin, M.A., Linda Stoyer, C.A.C, Xiomara M. Santos, M.S.W., Dr. David O'Connell, Dr. Philip Tietbohl, Dr. Loretta Martin-Halpine, and my seminar attendees. A special thanks to my literary agent, Sherrill Chidiac; to Barbara Karesh-Stender, who helped name this book in her sweet southern way; and to Renee (Young) Royer, who contributed many lively conversations to this book.

From the Author

This book portrays decent women in a good light. As *Nasty Men* is not a men-bashing book, *Nasty Women* is not a women-bashing book. I hope that it will clear up some of the major misunderstandings among men and women, and women and women. Sometimes women are not being nasty; they are just being women. We know from all the latest books on gender differences that men and women think and respond very differently about both the small things and the big picture. During the past decade, some good books on gender differences have been written. Since opening my practice in 1976, I have had numerous opportunities to see these gender differences in action, and as a result I have developed the observations I share in this book.

For more than two years, I was a psychologist for a prison. I evaluated and treated some very nasty women as well as some who were horrendously abused. Additionally, for five years, I was a consultant at the Caron Foundation, one of the top drug and alcohol facilities in the country. I have had the opportunity to evaluate more than three thousand women for mental health problems, substance abuse issues, and personality disorders. I have lectured nationally and internationally on relationships since 1977, having appeared on more than one hundred call-in shows on national television and radio discussing *Nasty People* and *Nasty Men.* I have been an expert witness in criminal, domestic, and custody cases. In my private practice, the majority of my clients have been women of many lifestyles, cultures, and positions in society. I have good friendships with women in my field who have contributed to this book. I also give seminars around the United States for thousands of therapists, counselors, social workers, and psychologists. So the material in this book comes from feedback from male and female therapists, male and female psychologists, women clients, professional men, and male clients.

Plenty of books have been written about men, mostly by women, and not all of them attempt to be balanced or to further the understanding of the sexes. However, you will not find many self-help books about women written by a man, which might go along with a certain widespread male gender mentality to avoid feelings and to not complain. Of course, I am generalizing, and understanding and communication are getting better, but a lot of work still needs to be done. Men have been taught not to complain, while women have been given the OK by society to vent (except for their feelings of anger).

A personal issue helped motivate me to write this book. My parents divorced when I was fifteen. I was very close to my mother and took her side. I remember my mother criticizing my father before, during, and after the divorce. I believed what she said; after all, she was my mother and she surely loved me. Then, when I was thirty, it struck me. My father never said one bad word about my mother and there *were* things he could have said. As much as I loved her, she was not perfect. With this realization, my respect for my father was amplified greatly.

Have I decided to write *Nasty Women* because my mother ruined me? No! I believe it needed to be written, and I think I have been able to write it in the most loving way possible so that men and women can better understand one another. I am sure I could discuss this book with my mother (if she were still alive), and I know that she would have wanted me to write it. I strongly believe women's intent is basically good (with some exceptions, of course). While men may not understand women, it is also true that women do not understand men as well as they may think they do.

Some women are tired of making the effort to understand men only to have to meet a man on *his* mental territory. This doesn't work anyway, as it just enables a man. Women also need to learn to deal with nasty women. Women do not understand all other women, and they can gain insight into those whose temperaments may be different from their own.

In *My Enemy, My Love*, Judith Levine acknowledges that some degree of misandry (man hating) exists almost universally among Western (American and European) women. Could it be that the man of today is paying the price for previous generations of male dominance and abuse?

This book describes gender-specific behavior of nasty women. A nasty woman could be any woman who uses controlling, punishing, or manipulative behavior. Nastier women would be someone like the Queen of Mean who makes all of her staff miserable and is unethical in her behavior. The nastiest woman would be someone like the one in Pennsylvania who murdered five husbands with a painful and undetectable poison that made them all suffer for months before they died.

In the process of writing *Nasty Women*, I made the most amazing discovery. I stumbled upon the main reason that marriages in Western society break up. I have presented this process to thousands of therapists in my seminars (psychologists, counselors, social workers, marriage and family therapists, and so forth) and it has been well received with amazement. This simple process has been overlooked for centuries. It is not a simple fact, but a big picture. The only reference to this process is a couple thousand years old. I am not a religious fanatic or Bible thumper by any means, but a documented process from the Bible was the final piece of the puzzle. I added this piece to the latest information from gender books and counseling techniques and the whole picture was formed, as you will see.

If I *have* uncovered the process for the deterioration of committed-mate relationships, then this book's value increases exponentially beyond the price you paid. This big picture should add greatly to the quality of your life. The rest of the book is pretty cool too, though. Happy sailing!

Introduction

Your pain is the breaking of the shell that encloses your understanding.
—THE PROPHET, KAHLIL GIBRAN, 1923

This book is a process, not an end product, which is good because you can take it with you and it unfolds. I want you to start here and read the Introduction so you get all the goods and the whole process.

I was asked to write *Nasty Women* five times, and I turned down the offer four times. To some, it seemed like a good follow-up to *Nasty People* and *Nasty Men*. I refused because I have the highest regard for women and I have always put them on a pedestal. I always believed them to be more trustworthy, caring, loving, and concerned. Most of the requests to write *Nasty Women* came from women who have read my books. I have received more than 3,500 letters, but I didn't want to write a book that might be "gender polarizing." I did not want to be involved in antifeminism or women bashing, and I didn't want to contribute to the wedge between the sexes. The chasm between men and women is wide enough, and I see it every day in my psychology practice.

While entertaining the idea of writing this book, I wondered who would buy a book called *Nasty Women*. It occurred to me that such a book might speak to at least five types of people:

1. Men who felt disenchanted by women and needed to understand them better
2. Women who wanted to know why some women are mean to other women
3. Women who wanted to understand how men become disenchanted
4. Women who perceive themselves as nasty but don't want to be
5. Women who would like a man to read about some *really* nasty women and realize what a good woman he has (and to be thankful he is not having a relationship with one of the nasty ones)

Are you ready to start the process? OK.

First, let's talk about *temperament*. We are all born equal in spirit, but each of us has a different temperament or basic inherited constitution. Some women dislike men and this is exhibited in a destructive way. They are called *misandrists*, just as women-hating men are called *misogynists*. Some of these women have tactics that are meant to kill a man's very soul, which I plan to expose along with the reasons behind them. Of course, a woman doesn't just wake up and arbitrarily say to herself, "I think I'll hate men from now on." There are *reasons*, and this information may benefit women who do not understand these other women.

Most healthy women tend to see the potential in a man and try to develop it within him. She wants to help him be the man she knows he can be. Much of the time, this is misunderstood and not appreciated by him. Her efforts conflict with a man's general attitude, which is one of acceptance. A man likes to be accepted, and he usually accepts other men (right or wrong) and only complains when something really bothers him and he feels he has to do something about it. So, early in the relationship, when his mate brings up his faults, he moves into action to fix them. Meanwhile, she keeps trying to make a better man out of him by coming up with more "areas of improvement." He begins to think that he will never be accepted. He feels that he can never please her, so he throws in the towel and becomes emotionally distant (trying to avoid the pain of facing his shortcomings and inadequacies). Her intent is good; his intent is good. But the misunderstanding causes one of the worst downward spirals of a marriage. Their marriage starts circling the commode and they don't realize why. This will be covered in depth later.

The organization of this book is similar to *Nasty Men*. One of my female friends came up with the idea of the vast sea for categorizing women. I was impressed with her ability to poke fun in a nonderogatory manner. If you have a sense of humor, you will enjoy reading further. Briefly, I have categorized behavior patterns in the following ways and will elaborate in later chapters. Consider this to be your preview to the women in the sea of life explained in more detail in Chapter 2.

- **The Flounder (Ms. Unpredictable):** You never know which side of her you will see in her personal relationships. One side seems to adore her mate and builds him up. The other side treats him like he is the lowest of the low. Life with her is a roller coaster, and he never knows when the next heart-stopping drop may come.
- **The Blowfish (Ms. Bullee):** She is unpredictable and one never knows when she is going to explode or why she goes off. When she blows, she shakes up the whole emotional stability of the household or workplace.
- **The Piranha (Ms. Bullee-Tootoo):** In the real world, the piranha is small, voracious, and hunts in schools and attacks any animal. Ms. Bullee-Tootoo follows the lead of the blowfish bully, verbally and emotionally feeding on the victim selected by the blowfish.
- **The Shark (Ms. Eetcha):** The shark will glide through the water with that shark smile on her face and those conscienceless eyes. She won't eat anyone if she's not hungry, but if she is, she will snap off an extremity before her victim even knows what happened. It's not that she deliberately sets out to hurt anyone; it was just dinnertime.

- **The Bottom Dweller (Ms. O. B. Livious):** The bottom dweller hangs out with losers. She can be wonderful to her abusive drug-dealing boyfriend, yet she won't give a decent guy a chance. Despite her looks and potential, she doesn't feel good enough.
- **The Surface Dweller (Ms. Skimmy):** Ms. Skimmy hangs out with people near the surface where it's sunny. If her man starts to sink, she is off looking for another surface dweller. She is an opportunist. She will seduce another woman's guy, even her best friend's, right out from underneath her. *Love* and *true* are four-letter words to her.
- **The Octopus (Ms. Doña Juanita):** The octopus juggles several men at once. She pulls in codependent (i.e., addicted to dysfunctional relationships) men who are hopelessly in love with her or are wanna-be boyfriends and has a lot of men who are "just friends." She uses them and the men actually like it.
- **The Eel (Ms. Dependent):** The eel latches onto a host and doesn't let go. She is known to hang on to the point of death and no amount of pain or suffering will detach her. To a pathological degree, she cannot be an individual.
- **The Sponge (Ms. Codependent):** The sponge is similar to the eel. She is dependent . . . or more like codependent. She absorbs abuse and cushions her codependent object from reality, enabling him or her to actively participate in his or her addictions (drinking, sex, drugs, overworking, overeating, and so forth). She looks like a saint compared to her addict counterpart. She is unconsciously supporting and enabling the downfall of her mate or friend.

- **The Corporate Bullhead (Ms. Anal-izer):** She goes by the rules. She is not personable and no fun to work for. People better live up to her impossible expectations, or she will be hostile in a covertly cordial professional way. She will never be satisfied and will not acknowledge anyone. She doesn't know the meaning of the word *supportive*.

Nasty women can be sharks, surface dwellers, octopuses, or other characters depending on their traits. These categories expose tactics of manipulation, punishment, and control that nasty women use. Some women use these tactics because they were done to them or they saw Mom using them on Dad. Some of these women are selfish and manipulate for self-gain. Some have little or no conscience. Some nasty women in the corporate world feel that they have to act like men (as they perceive them to be) to accomplish their promotional goals. Some are men haters, women haters, general haters, misled, or unconscionable. Most are just caught up in dysfunction. Their motivations and the reasons behind them are exposed in this book.

There are many dwellers in the sea of life. These are but a few of the ones that you would not want to see marry your brother or close friend.

Misunderstanding

Chapter 1 describes the many ways that women are misunderstood and how men interpret these misunderstandings (thereby providing some understanding of men too). One woman might not choose her words wisely, attacking her paramour's self-esteem when she just wants to get her feelings heard. Another woman perhaps "tests" her mate by making statements she doesn't really mean. He does not understand these "tests" and interprets them as character flaws in himself or her deliberate infliction of unnecessary pain and suffering upon him. The chapter defines the intent of a misunderstood woman and how to interpret her behavior, words, and feelings appropriately.

What to Do

Men and women can learn how to deal with women who appear to be nasty but are not. For example, women who have been battered or sexually abused tend to insult men, without meaning to, by their reactions to them. They may react as if men are dangerous to them, and a sensitive man may feel as if she is treating him as if he is a monster. Men need to learn how to work and interact with these women without taking their reactions personally. Chapter 3 will help show how by providing the following:

- Understanding (the cure for *mis*understanding)
- Examples of difficult situations and the successful responses
- Pointers that seem to work in most situations

That's right! Sometimes you need to just leave the situation. Sometimes there is no other way . . . after you have tried your best. Just as there is no cure for certain diseases, there is also no cure for certain psychological situations.

The Big Picture

I have coined the phrase *situational awareness*, which means the **content** of the context is not so much the problem as the **context** (situation) itself. If your boss is a misandrist or misogynist, the *situation* is the problem, not any particular *event*. If a woman says, "You either give up that friendship with George or our marriage," a pattern may be emerging. Perhaps she doesn't want her husband to have a friend—period. If George is a decent friend and this situation arises frequently, a good response might be, "From now on, I am not going to choose between you and my friend."

Taking It Personally

In dealing with nasty women or men, it is important to remember two concepts. The first one is that you need to remain situationally aware. The second one is to not take things personally.

Eighty-five percent of the time, the conflict or reaction isn't personal. Does that mean people should stand aside and analytically look from afar? No. That would be impersonal. Let me explain. When we are children, we take *everything* personally. We think the moon actually follows us down the street. For example, my little boy told me he would like to stay up all night sometime. Then his six- year-old mind thought about it for a minute and he said, "Dad, if I stay up all night long, will the sun still come up in the morning?" He thought the sun revolved around his activities.

As adults, we sometimes mistakenly take situations personally. One time I was in a Kmart and a teenaged salesgirl threw my change at me. In this situation I had a few choices.

1. I could have picked up my change without saying anything and walked out, in which case my whole day might have been about the Kmart clerk and what I should have said or done.
2. I could have gotten upset and yelled at her because she may have reminded me of someone in the past who treated me badly.
3. I could have complained to her manager and possibly gotten her fired.

Instead of taking her actions personally, I remained situationally aware. She didn't know me, and I was just the next customer. I saved all that energy by not allowing my buttons to be pushed. I looked into the eyes of a sixteen-year-old girl and what came out of my mouth was, "Are you having a bad day?" She burst into tears and told me her boyfriend had just broken up with her. I remembered that she was on the phone when I came in and realized that she must have just hung up with him. It *wasn't* personal. Should I have been annoyed that she threw my change at me?

Yes. Was she the person in my past who treated me badly? No. Did she need to be fired? Probably not. Was it about me? No. Did I have enough situational awareness to get involved? Yes. I wasn't impersonal, and I didn't take it personally.

So here are the answers in dealing with nasty women:

1. Don't take things personally, but don't be impersonal.
2. Maintain a situational awareness. Don't let your buttons get pushed.

We will be fine-tuning these responses throughout this book.

Is the woman you were thinking of when you bought this book nasty? Maybe. Should you take her behavior personally? No. Should you respond? Yes (after you turn down the "personal" button intensity by 85 percent). There is an 85 percent chance that a misunderstanding is at work or her buttons are being pushed or your buttons are being pushed. As you read on, you will learn how to react during these situations along with how to cope with bonafide nasty women you may encounter.

MISUNDERSTANDINGS

What paineth thee in others in thyself must be.
—WILLIAM SHAKESPEARE

Women often think they know men, because they know a man's feelings, sometimes better than he does. Knowing feelings and interpreting the source of those feelings are two separate and very different things. One of the things that men get most upset about is when a woman attributes incorrect ulterior motives to a man's behavior, or his feelings. That's where the phrase "she just doesn't understand me" comes from. She loses her credibility in his eyes, and she feels that she lost him, somewhere.

A misunderstanding is when you think you know something about someone, but you really don't. Misunderstandings may make a woman appear nasty to men, even when the woman may actually have the best of intentions. People know when they don't understand something, but they don't realize when they *mis*understand something. That's when they think they understand but don't really understand. This misunderstanding is the major cause of war and divorce.

The Jujube Doll

In this chapter, I am going to generalize about men and women. I realize I am doing this and what I am about to say does not fit every man or every woman. Nevertheless, when I present this information to psychologists, social workers, and counselors, they find it fascinating and worthwhile. If you have read some of the gender books, you may find some of this familiar. I will present new material, but what I really want you to see is the bigger picture. To help, I will present it by updating a chart, just as I do in my seminars. That way you will not lose the bigger picture because of some of the interesting details. OK? Here we go.

Most women do not realize the influence that they have with men. Some do and use it wisely. Some do and use it manipulatively. Most women use it without realizing it.

The Bible says that a man cleaves to his mother; then he leaves his mother and cleaves to his wife. I never really understood the cleaving thing until now. Let's take a look at it.

Self-Esteem

Who is a man *with* the first five years of his life during his most important developmental periods? Yes, his mother. So where does he get his self-esteem during those years? Yes . . . a woman. The hand that rocks the cradle has shaped this world more than any other influence. In many ways women have held the reins in the background. While the stallion pulls the buggy, the woman has kept him on the road by tugging on the reins. All the while, she encourages him, "You're doing it, Honey!" Most of the time, it can be called synchronicity or teamwork.

A woman also gets her self-esteem from her mother, but she identifies with the mother; a man cannot. Whereas a woman *becomes* her mother in certain ways, a man wants to be *becoming* to his mother so she is proud of him. He is separate, but connected. Back to cleaving.

When a man meets a woman whom he wants to share his life with, he drops his self-esteem, or his jujube doll, in her lap—not his whole self-esteem, but that part that belongs to a woman. He does this unconsciously. Afterward, what this woman thinks of him becomes very important to him. At the beginning of their relationship, he may try to fix anything she is dissatisfied with. If she doesn't like something about him, he takes care of it. She may think that he does this because he loves her, and indirectly that may be true. But primarily, he makes these changes because she holds his self-esteem in her lap, and if she sticks a pin in that jujube doll, it really hurts.

For the most part, she doesn't know this is going on in his mind and emotions. She doesn't look at it that way at all. She doesn't know she is the keeper of his self-esteem (jujube doll).

To complicate things, women hardly ever marry a man for who he is. She marries him for his . . . potential. When a woman meets a man, he becomes her home-improvement project.

Men	Women
Self-Esteem	Home Improvement Project

She wants to make him a better man. So she comes up with some improvements he could make (he may view them as her "dissatisfactions"). She doesn't realize she has his self-esteem in her lap, so when she rises up, it falls on the floor. She may inadvertently step on it and kick it out of the way. A man is a fixer of problems, whereas a woman is an improver of persons.

The self-esteem she holds (his jujube doll) takes a beating with her "dissatisfaction" (in his eyes). She accidentally steps on the jujube doll and the self-esteem says, "Ouch!" Over the years, he may improve, according to her recommendations, but he becomes slower and slower to respond. Then one day, she inadvertently steps on the jujube doll with her spiked heels, and it is so painful for him that he takes his self-esteem back. He stops cleaving, and that's the day that she loses a significant amount of influence. He tries to make himself not care what she thinks. She experiences this as emotional distance and is afraid that he may not love her anymore. All this for trying to make him a better man and for being unaware of the jujube doll, which she never agreed to take care of in the first place.

Acceptance vs. Involvement

We know that men like *acceptance*, maybe even to a fault.

Joe and Harry are driving down the road. Joe says to Harry, "Harry, I cheated on my wife last night." Harry responds, "Gosh, Joe, you have to be careful. You have a nice wife there. You could mess up your whole family." But the underlying message that Harry gives Joe is this: "Joe, even if you're a serial killer, I am your friend to the end." Total acceptance is there.

Women aren't like that. Rose and Sylvia are driving down the road and Rose says to Sylvia, "I cheated on my husband last night." Sylvia gets upset, "You WHAT!? What is wrong with you? You could mess everything up!" There is no acceptance there, but there is . . . involvement. Women get involved. Men are not so personally involved as to appear to be interfering.

Men	Women
Self-Esteem	Home Improvement Project
Acceptance	Involvement

Intent vs. Feelings

The gender books say that men are 80 percent words in their expression of things and 20 percent feelings. Women are 20 percent words and 80 percent feelings in their expression of things. Even though women are usually more verbal, they are expressing *feelings* verbally. Many men just don't think feelings are very important and they need to learn that feelings are important . . . to her.

The seat of a woman's soul is her feelings. A woman usually feels you know *her* if you know her feelings.

Men	Women
Self-Esteem	Home Improvement Project
Acceptance	Involvement
80% Words; 20% Feelings	80% Feelings; 20% Words
	Feelings

However, this is not true for a man. The seat of a man's soul is usually not his feelings. It is his intent or purpose. We raise men this way in our society. We *affirm* that feelings are not important. "Don't be a baby. Be a man!" He makes his intent or purpose more important . . . just like we taught him.

Herein lies another major misunderstanding. A woman may keep trying to get a man to share his feelings. She believes they can have more intimacy that way. That's not necessarily true, although there are some men who think that their feelings are the seat of their soul. Mostly, a man shares himself and who he is by sharing his hopes and

Men	Women
Self-Esteem	Home Improvement Project
Acceptance	Involvement
80% Words; 20% Feelings	80% Feelings; 20% Words
Intent/Purpose	Feelings

dreams. He might say, "Well, I know I may have messed up, but here's what I really wanted for us and our family." Meanwhile, she might respond, "You are just rationalizing and making excuses. If you would just share your feelings with me, once in a while, we could have a more intimate relationship." When she says that, it makes him realize, "She doesn't understand me." (There's that phrase again.)

Now, it could be true that he *is* rationalizing and making excuses, but maybe not. If he isn't, then he was baring his soul to a deaf ear. She missed out on exactly what she was seeking from him (intimacy through vulnerability).

She has a similar problem when she tries to make her feelings known. Maybe she has a job that she enjoys, but she comes home every night complaining about her boss, just to vent her feelings. After a couple weeks of this, he may say to her, "Get a new job, already!" She doesn't want to get a new job. She was just baring her soul to her mate, and it fell on deaf ears. She doesn't feel heard.

Besides whatever genetics may be involved, our society teaches boys to be goal oriented and suppress their feelings.

Society teaches girls to look for the feelings. Women seem to know that the *way* to the goal is just as important as the goal itself.

The Bigger Picture

So let's look at the bigger picture.

1. She is trying to make him a better man and points out the areas of improvement he needs to make to be all he can be. Meanwhile, he perceives that she doesn't accept him the way he is. No matter what he does, he can't seem to please this woman.

2. He is trying to make her understand where he is coming from (intent, purpose) and she is trying to get him to acknowledge her feelings. He says things like, "You are overreacting." She says things like, "Cut the crap and just tell me how you feel."

3. He takes her words literally and generally and takes a hit to his self-esteem when she tries to express her feelings. He may try to correct her when she doesn't have the details right. She gets frustrated because he gets caught up in the words and doesn't see that she needs him to see her feelings, which he doesn't acknowledge. He doesn't think feelings are important. She doesn't think his words are important. I call this the XY Syndrome, as suggested by one of my seminar attendees.

Let's take a concrete example. A woman calls her husband at work and tells him to bring home a quart of milk.

He says OK, but men don't like to be told what to do. She is not actually telling him what to do (like a power thing). She just assumes he wants to participate in the relationship, so she assumes he will bring home the milk. Due to his semiconscious internal conflict, he comes home without the milk. She asks, "Did you get the milk?" "Oh," he says, "I forgot."

Now she is upset because he obviously doesn't want to participate in the relationship, so she says, "You are *so* irresponsible!" It really hurts his feelings to think that this woman who should know him by now thinks of him as "irresponsible" after all the responsible things he has done. What does a man do when he gets his feelings hurt? He usually gets angry. So he says, "Oh yeah?! Well, you didn't think I was irresponsible last month when I put the down payment on your new car, did ya?! And you didn't think I was irresponsible every single month for the past ten years when I wrote out the mortgage check, did ya?!" He is all red in the face and his eyes are bulging. He is upset (after all the responsible things he has done) that one little slip with a quart of milk wipes away all his efforts. He is too involved in defending his jujube doll to see her feelings. For her part, she doesn't mean that he is irresponsible *in general*. She just thinks he is irresponsible specifically for not getting the milk. Being a word-oriented creature, he takes it literally and generally. It felt like a big hit to his self-esteem, but it wasn't meant that way. He still hasn't acknowledged her feelings, and he is getting into a discussion about responsibility, which isn't the point at all. Now she is *really* upset! He is trying to win the argument instead of acknowledging her. So now she is going to try to remember all the times he was ever irresponsible in his entire life. If she is not going to get her feelings acknowledged, then at least she is going to win and be "right."

After several years of this, they bring their marriage into my office (the DMZ—demilitarized zone). He usually comes in after she insists upon it. He seems apathetic and doesn't hold much hope. So I bring him in first and ask, "What do you think the problem is?"

He usually says something like, "She doesn't accept me for who I am, and no matter what I do, I can never please this woman." I might ask him, "What do you think your wife thinks of you now as compared to when you first got married?" He says, "Oh, when we first got married, she thought I was a god. Now she thinks I am a loser." I bring her in and ask her, "What do you think of your husband now, as compared to when you were first married?"

She may respond, "Oh, when we first got married, he was a slob, ignorant, and irresponsible. He is much better now."

He looks at her and his mouth drops in surprise.

Do you see how the bigger picture fits (or doesn't fit) together? Do you see why he perceives her as nasty (e.g., nags, doesn't understand me, never pleased, doesn't accept me, etc.)? Do you see why he has become emotionally distant (i.e., taken back his jujube doll so he doesn't feel the pain)? Do you see why she is upset and mis-emotional (i.e., she has held in her feelings until she is ready to burst)? Why she feels worthless to him (never getting her feelings acknowledged)? Why he feels worthless in her eyes (perceiving that she thinks he is never good enough)?

Are they invalidating each other? Without realizing it, they are. But they don't understand each other. They can't put themselves in the other one's place (and follow the golden rule) because they misunderstand each other. It is fairly easy to put yourself in another's place as yourself. It is much harder to put yourself in another's place as the other person.

Let me explain that further. In the first two years of his marriage, a man regularly bought his wife carnations. She approached him one day and said, "I don't mean to seem ungrateful, but why do you buy me carnations?"

He said, "Well, they smell good and last a long time."

Then she said, "Yes, and I like carnations, but did you know what flower *I* like best?"

At that moment he realized how narcissistic he had been. She said, "*I* like roses. Red roses."

He was a *good* narcissist, but still a narcissist. He tried to put himself in her place . . . as him. And *he* liked carnations. It is much harder to put yourself in someone else's place as that person.

So what is the problem here? Misunderstanding. Then what is the cure? Well, if you were following me through this explanation, you already have the big part of it. Simply . . . understanding is the cure for misunderstanding. That's the good news.

If you have related to the aforementioned, then you have just gotten the chicken soup (penicillin). Do you feel cured right after you take penicillin? No. It's a process, not a magic wand from a fairy tale.

One thing. Once a man understands that a woman has good intentions, he can relate. He has to be reminded of her intent (i.e., it wouldn't hurt to stroke the jujube doll after stepping on it). It is a well-known and effective management technique to tell employees how valued they are before giving a criticism. That paints the bigger picture before giving a negative detail. It prevents a person from making a mountain out of a molehill. It puts things into perspective. A man can go downhill pretty fast if he gets a poor self-image. So we need to paint the whole image, not just the negative piece.

Neither men nor women like to be dissed (disrespected). An interesting thing I learned while preparing the manuscript for this book was that women don't like to be called names. They don't usually like names like the "b" word. It's an image thing. Men seem to be OK with name-calling like, "Hey dumbass." However, they hate names like "irresponsible, immature, and ignorant." If you call a man a jerk, he will know you are probably angry. Men call each other pet names in adolescence like "a-hole," and they learn to tolerate it and even think it's funny. Women who are called irresponsible by a friend might not take it so personally. Actually it is *all* name-calling. It is still labeling a person whether you call them the "b" word, jerk, or irresponsible.

Like I said, *exposing* what is actually happening is the fix. Women like this fix because it acknowledges what is happening, and men like it because it is a fix. The woman can then choose whether she wants to be caretaker for the jujube doll. She may say, "Hey, I never agreed to take care of your self-esteem. That's not my job." That could work. The man can find this to be a reasonable arrangement once it is out in the open. However, a woman loses a lot of influence that way.

Another approach is one in which the woman says, "I am sorry I have stepped all over your self-esteem. Now I can see all the spiked heel marks in your jujube doll. I will take better care of it in the future." If this is the approach she is willing to take, then I will suggest this: when he pulls up in the driveway without the milk, stroke the jujube doll first. First, let him know how you feel in general (in the bigger picture). "I can't believe you forgot the milk . . . a man as responsible as you are, who bought me a new car last month and hasn't missed a mortgage payment for ten years." Now you have stroked the jujube doll to immense proportions. The jujube doll is so big now that the man has to live up to this image. He will probably jump back in his car and run off to get that milk. Although this could be perceived as a little manipulative, I don't know any man that minds being manipulated this way. Actually, this tactic is more of an acknowledgment rather than a manipulation.

I could also tell the woman to choose her words more wisely. She could just say directly, "I am really angry you didn't get the milk." There would be no arguments about responsibility. I don't say this to women these days, because women have been trying to adapt their mentality to a man's mentality for centuries and it hasn't worked to either's benefit. It only enables him. He never learns to look for the feelings.

Instead of that, I will ask the man how his wife said it when she said he was irresponsible. He may say, "She looked at me viciously and said, 'You are soooooo irresponsible!'"

"Did you notice any *feeling* in that?" I ask.

He is taken aback a little but admits there was a lot of feeling in what she said. I add, "Perhaps if you said something like, 'Wow, you are really angry about that.'"

She might be so happy that he finally acknowledged one of her feelings that she would jump in the car and go get the milk herself (but probably not).

When I ask the man what made him so upset when she said he was irresponsible, I might get this: "Well, it really hurt me to think that she thinks that way of me. I mean, after all the responsible things I have ever done, to have it all count for nothing just because I forgot a quart of milk." You see how different the thinking is between men and women?

I don't like to beat this one example to death, but if you can see all the elements here, then you may see the bigger picture of how this can be applied to so many interactions.

Intimacy

A woman may think that she doesn't want to be his "mom," so she is reluctant to acknowledge her influence on his self-esteem. In that case, she shouldn't have married him for his potential, thinking she would improve him. There is a big difference between having self-esteem and having an ego. Pumping up the ego is enabling and patronizing. The acknowledgment of someone's positive qualities is good for acknowledging who that person is. This accepts a person and acknowledges his or her self-esteem, and that produces intimacy. By the same token, a man who placates a woman's feelings does her no justice. It is his way of patronizing her. A man who acknowledges her feelings and sees who she is creates intimacy. Intimacy is different for each. Intimacy is a man listening to her feelings while she is listening to his hopes and dreams. Intimacy for a man is when his wife helps him wash the car and watches "Monday Night Football" with him while ordering out for pizza. In turn (and in a reciprocal relationship, there needs to be an "in turn") might be when a man spends time with his wife and just listens and acknowledges what she is telling him without trying to fix it or react defensively to what she says. I don't mean that every man likes to watch "Monday Night Football" or that every woman likes to just hang out and talk. I hope you get what I am saying about what produces intimacy. It is when you show enough interest in someone to know him or her and then give what he or she most desires or needs to receive.

If the misunderstandings of the XY Syndrome go on for years, they undermine the marriage. Stuck in this syndrome, the man believes that whatever he does is never good enough for his wife. He can never seem to please her. He always feels a deficit in himself in her eyes. He believes she doesn't accept him for who he is. She doesn't understand him, otherwise she wouldn't think he was such a piece of junk. He experiences her as being dissatisfied and nagging and viewing him as a lesser person than he is. He believes she attributes lesser motives to what he does. Ultimately, he throws in the towel emotionally and moves to protect the jujube doll from being stepped on. When he takes back the jujube doll, he takes the emotional connections of intimacy that really belong to the marriage. He divorces her or separates from her emotionally, even though he may remain in the same house.

At that point, the woman usually senses something has changed and asks him to go to counseling with her. She has put so much effort into the relationship that she can't understand what has gone wrong. In turn, he also feels that he has put effort into the relationship trying to fix things and satisfy her by trying to do what she wants. He feels hopeless, because it looks like he has failed to be what she wants. Around this time, he may be drawn to other women who seem to like him for who he is, but they too are just seeing his potential, and the whole syndrome starts over again, possibly leaving an exhausted and resentful ex-wife and a family without a father.

None of this can be proved scientifically except by survey research. One must take a phenomenological approach that reflects people's experiences, perceptions, and opinions. You have to decide whether this is true for you or not. Science is very concrete and therefore limited. It can help you only with things that can be measured. Self-esteem, love, and nurturing grow out of the human spirit and cannot be measured. Science is a wonderful thing, but it is concrete and not the bigger picture.

A phenomenological approach that includes science makes up the bigger picture I have been writing about. In this book, it is the bigger picture that is important for you to see. You need your prefrontal lobe for that. I hope you can stay in your prefrontal lobe for the rest of the book. That's the part of you that sees the bigger picture. It's that part that enables you to imagine the consequences of your actions. It's the captain's chair of your life—where you are surrounded by windows so you can see where you have been and where you are going.

Let me remind you again. It's nice to understand the interesting details of the XY Syndrome. But the big picture is important because it shows how marriages are destroyed by misunderstandings, which decimate the bond and intimacy couples have. If you see the bigger picture, I am sure that knowledge will kick the devil in the ass and I like to do that whenever I can.

2

NASTY WOMEN

To thine own self be true.
—William Shakespeare

Why are some women nasty? It may be because these nasty women have some of the following qualities. They could be:

- Territorial
- Dominating
- Chemically imbalanced
- Misunderstanding something
- Misunderstood
- Uncaring about others
- Narcissistic
- Manipulative
- Unconscionable
- Harboring feelings of superiority to others (a legend in their own mind)

In the past, they may have been:

- Physically abused
- Emotionally abused
- Sexually abused
- Neglected
- Traumatized
- Raised dysfunctionally
- Trained to behave that way

You may be thinking that it is always a choice to be nasty. So what if they had bad things happen to them? Why do they have to take it out on everyone else? Let's clear this one up first. I have two stories for you.

I was stung by bees when I was four years old. I don't like to use myself as an example, but I am the only person I can immediately get permission from to use the story. I don't remember the bee incident. It wasn't that it was such a trauma that I lost the memory. It's just that I don't remember anything about being four. (Our cognitive memory doesn't kick in until we are about five. As soon as you can call yourself "I," your cognitive memory has become developed enough to use.) Anyway, my father remembers the bees and so does my body (the mammal part of me). My father told me I stepped into a bees' nest and ran down to our farmhouse. Of course, when you run, the bees sting you more.

Here's what happens at the beginning of summer now that I'm an adult. I might be sitting at a picnic table and a bee will buzz near my ear and fly in front of my eye. Then what happens is a very dissociative experience. In less than a moment my mind says, "Oh no! Here we go again." My body jumps up from the picnic table. My mind is saying, "Gee, I hope I don't knock over the picnic table." Just then my knee comes up with two or three times its normal strength, thanks to the adrenaline that is now in my bloodstream.

My leg knocks over the picnic table, and the potato salad and hamburgers go flying in the grass. My body then starts running for an open space. I say to myself, "This is stupid. If I run, the bees are liable to sting me more."

But my body doesn't give a darn what I think. It just starts running. I hope to myself that my wife isn't too upset that I knocked over the picnic table, but out of my peripheral vision, I can see her standing with her hands on her hips and a scowl on her face. Now I know I am in for it when I get back. My body keeps running until there is no evidence of bees. Then I have to walk it back. This is all due to my bee trauma, of which I have no recollection. Can you relate to this?

Now I will tell you the second story, and it may be hard to relate to until you hear the whole story. I was at a county prison (as a staff member, of course), and I was asked to counsel a woman who seemed to have a lot of potential but kept defeating herself. I had two sessions to cure her. I will call her Mary.

She was a very tall woman and seemed very sweet. This was her third time in jail for assault. I asked her what the problem was. She said, "The problem is that I can't come to jail anymore." I told her I would notify the authorities and let them know that she couldn't come here anymore. She laughed and said, "It's like this. Every time I come to jail I lose my job and my apartment, and I have to get my relatives to watch my kids. I can't do this anymore. You have to help me."

I told her I would try and asked her how she got in jail this time. She said she punched out her forelady (boss). I asked why, and she said, "Because she got in my face."

"OK, but *why* did you hit her?" I asked. She gave me the chicken neck stance and looked at me. "I told you," she said, "She got in my face." I started feeling cynical about being able to help her. I told her that people get in my face all the time and I don't punch them out. She said, "Well, I do!"

"Why?" I asked.

"I don't know," she said, "That's why I came to see you."

I said, "OK. Why were you here the last time?"

"I punched out my landlady," she said.

"Why?"

"Because she got in my face."

"Oh . . . 'K. How about the first time you came to jail?"

"I punched out my neighbor."

I said, "Let me guess. It was a woman."

"Right."

"And she got in your face."

"Yeah, how'd you know?"

"They teach us to read minds in graduate school."

We both laughed.

To make a long (but necessary) story shorter, we talked about her mother. Evidently, her father got her mother pregnant at the same time he got his mistress pregnant. They both went to the hospital on the same day and had their babies the same day. Her mother chose to believe that the babies were mixed up at the hospital and that Mary was actually the mistress's baby. So, when Mary was a little girl, and her father would go to the mistress's house, Mary's mother would start ranting and raving. She would say awful things to her like, "You are just like your father. You are no good. I don't know why I put up with you. You are not even my kid!" Her mother would shake her and get in her face. And then her mother would beat her to unconsciousness.

Of course, this traumatized her, much like my bee trauma, but much worse. We know how physical abuse gets passed on from one generation to another. A rageful parent takes out that rage on a child. That child then becomes fearful. What is fear? Fear can actually be suppressed rage. Sometimes fear is "rage held back." We are programmed by nature for "survival of the fittest," and the way nature does this is that we "become" (momentarily) the winner (survivor) (i.e., we do what the survivor did because the survivor is the fittest).

So here's what happened with the forelady:

1. The forelady started to rant and rave at Mary. Mary became fearful (suppressed rage was stirred up). She felt like she was in the same situation as with her mother. She felt helpless.
2. The forelady then got in her face. This triggered the body (the programmed human mammal) to switch to the winning/surviving stance. Adrenaline was released in Mary's system, giving her two or three times her normal strength and making her superfocused.
3. Mary switched into being her mother momentarily (the survivor, the one in control, the winner) and punched out the forelady.

How many times have you said, "I am never going to do this to *my* children"? And then you did it or at least had the impulse, didn't you? So could this woman help it? Could she stop herself from punching out a female authority figure who got in her face? Absolutely not. Human mammals as well as other mammals are programmed by instinct for hundreds of thousands of years to take on the winning stance (surviving personality). It is a momentary personality. How many times have you acted like your mom or your dad? You momentarily "became them" in emotionally charged situations.

Did the landlady, the forelady, and the neighbor each think this woman was nasty? Sure they did. All of them got knocked out cold. Did she ever punch out a man? No. A woman friend? No. As cynical as I was, at first, about her problem, I had to admit she couldn't help it. We covered all this in her first session! The second session had to "cure" her. I thought about it a lot over the next week. Could I send her to a place that cures PTSD (post-traumatic stress disorder)? No. How about EMDR (eye movement desensitization and reprocessing)? No money, no budget, no deal.

I ended up using a twelve-step process modified from the one used by Alcoholics Anonymous (AA). In AA, one of the primary steps is to admit you are powerless over alcohol. She was willing to admit that she was powerless over "authority figure women who get in her face." She was unable to control her reaction similar to the way an alcoholic can't resist alcohol. So, we decided that she shouldn't work for a female, if she could help it. We decided that she needed to leave whenever a woman got in her face. In her culture that could be perceived as cowardice, but she was able to rationalize it by realizing she was leaving to save that person from harm. She hasn't been back to jail in eight years, so I assume we were lucky enough to help her. Did we cure the trauma? No. If you are an authority figure woman and you manage to get in her face, you are in for a big surprise.

Taking It Personally

If you are an authority figure woman and you get in Mary's face, she will knock you out. It isn't personal. She would knock out *any* woman whom she saw as an authority figure who got in her face. I am not saying you should just lie down and be a victim. But why take on the additional burden of making it personal, when it isn't really? It's bad enough to be knocked unconscious, but then to think it was personal would add so much more emotional charge to it. I don't mean you should take it impersonally and objectively, either. Whether Mary can help it or not, she is still responsible for what she does. Nothing will improve until she takes responsibility for what she does, and does something about it. But nothing will improve by blaming her either.

Why do we take things personally? When we are children, we believe everything relates to us. We are narcissistic, but God makes us cute so that we don't get beatings. Try to remember, most of the time, it's not about *you*.

I was evaluating adolescent girls at a facility one night, and the next girl to be evaluated opened my door and stood frozen in my doorway. The human mammal part of her seemed to be scared and growling, while the intellectual side of her was contemplating something. I said, "Do I remind you of someone?"

She said, "Yes, but I don't want to talk about it." I said, "OK. Would you feel better if we left the door open?" She said she would. She sat down and said, "I don't want to talk about this, but you look like a neighbor of mine who fell in love with me when I was in third grade." This man was sent off to jail, and she ended up with the reputation of "the molested girl."

Should I have taken her reaction to me personally? If I did, we wouldn't have gotten very far. I didn't take it personally, but I didn't take it impersonally either. I showed concern and saw that she was having a reaction to something. I could have said, "What's *your* problem?" I could have said, "Get in here and sit down." Things would have gone much differently then. I know they would have, because there was a doctor who looked like me and she had to see him next. He was a gruff guy who was very busy. She had the same reaction to him, and he said, "Sit down and shut the door." She ended up tearing her blouse, running down the hall, and yelling, "Rape! Rape!" We knew he didn't do anything, but he was still pretty embarrassed. We don't have time for other people's hang-ups, aberrations, quirks, and so on. But there they are. Sometimes we end up spending more time dealing with people when we don't have time for them. People take it personally when you are impersonal.

The Sea of Life

On a female friend's advice, I have classified behavior patterns in the following ways based on the idea of the vast sea for characterizing patterns of attitude ('tudes) and behavior. This will enable you to see the big picture from your captain's chair.

The Flounder (Ms. Unpredictable)

In the sea, a flounder is a fish that is shaped differently from other fish. Its eyes are on the topside of its flat head. It swims sideways through its whole life with its eyes looking up from the bottom for nourishment.

Humans flounder when they have an intense fear that they will be abandoned. The flounder's reaction to this perceived abandonment is intense fear or volatile anger. She can be very manipulative. If her mate has to go away on a business trip, she may get sick the day he is supposed to leave, or she may accuse him of meeting another woman, or she may just beg him to stay home because she needs him. She feels desperate, and there is nothing more important to her than the resolution of her feelings at that moment. She is not looking at the potential long-term results of her manipulation. Her mate could lose a promotion, a raise, or the job itself.

She looks to him to fill the emptiness that she feels. If he does lose his job, she may feel insecure again and blame him for it. If he does stay home with her that day, she may still feel insecure and empty and fear her need for him. She has emotional extremes from "too happy" to anger to sadness. She may exhibit unpredictable and dangerous behavior, such as addictions to sex, alcohol, spending, gambling, or drugs. Sometimes she may have suicidal thoughts and behavior.

If the relationship has been going well, she may do something to cause chaos, strife, or a crisis. She may have an affair. When she is confronted with the affair, she may break down, become sorry, and beg for forgiveness. This will all be very intense and dramatic, the way one might expect an adolescent girl to act. In many ways, she has the emotional capacity of an adolescent girl, but with the full cognitive ability of a grown woman. That can make her very cunning and manipulative. It can also make her very interesting and fun. She is liable to cast her inhibitions to the wind and partake in the pleasure of the moment. At these times, she doesn't entertain thoughts about the long-term consequences of her actions. Her life is a series of fires that she jumps into or has to put out. There is always a crisis. Things are always intense to her. She seems to be stuck in the emotional world of an adolescent or preadolescent. Everything is black or white. Her mate is either the most wonderful person in the world or a nothing, depending on her mood or what he has done for her lately. He can't expect her to appreciate all the sacrifices he has made for her. She has little ability to see the bigger picture of things. It is always, "Yes, but what have you done for me lately?"

He may truly love her, but she cannot feel it and pushes him to prove it to her all the time. She can be arrogant and have a sense of entitlement while he is constantly trying to prove his love to her. Then when he gets fed up and backs away, she is like a little girl, grabbing onto his legs, begging him to stay, promising she will be good from then on.

In her family background, there may be moderate to severe abuse and neglect. Her siblings may not have had the same reaction to it as she did. Her way of being is probably a combination of the following:

1. Her particular temperament
2. Certain damaging environmental conditions (abuse, neglect)
3. Absence of nurturing during significant windows of development

For example, she may have been unlucky enough to have her mother be depressed at a time she really needed her developmentally, or maybe her father emotionally or physically abused her during a crucial developmental stage. With her particular temperament, the environment may have done more damage to her than if she had a different temperament (e.g., it's been shown that the absence of a parent during a crucial stage of development can cause separation anxiety). But she has a lot of exciting qualities, doesn't she? Her mate or friend may have gone along with her on her "cast fate to the wind" attitude, to the degree that he has done things that commit him to the relationship (marriage, children, business partnership, promises, agreements, etc.). Maybe he got caught up in her euphoria, or anger, or sadness. She might tend to pick someone responsible, someone who is the opposite of herself in many ways. And now, after some careless but exciting moments, he is stuck.

There are probably millions of flounders and therefore millions more people who are affected by them.

What can be done to fix this? Wrong question. Instead, a better question is, what can be done to *manage* it? There are some things, but her mate may be so overwhelmed and resentful that he cannot continue the relationship. Nonetheless, he feels trapped because this woman needs him, despises him, and feels she can't live without him.

This woman has what I call "family trauma." It is her early relationships that are causing her distress. She gets "triggered" by certain aspects of relationships. For example, she may be doing just fine without a man in her life, but when she gets involved in a relationship, she may turn into a woman with the characteristics I've described. Can she be fixed? Truthfully? I have seen it happen, but it is a long haul. Advancements in psychology have not reached a level yet where she can be treated efficiently and effectively. She is going to need a lot of emotional trauma work (vs. talk therapy). She cannot be fixed by her mate. He may be the responsible one who is connected to her. She may have a lot of redeeming qualities. It may be worth it for him to stay with her, but he can always expect some degree of the flounder characteristics.

What will work with her? Love. Tough love, like one would give to an adolescent girl, although this puts her mate in a parental role for the moment. And, she is not an adolescent girl but she does have the full cognitive ability of an adult. This makes it hard to deal with her. He has to respond to her adult side as well as her child side. For example, if she wants his car and he doesn't want to give it to her because he is afraid she will get inebriated or use it for a sexual encounter, he needs to say no. He does not need to tell her his fears—just say, no. She may berate him or threaten him with a tit-for-tat vengeful promise. He doesn't need to tell her why he made this decision, just stick to it. She will get over it the way an adolescent gets over it. He must always show love. She is used to people rejecting her without love. He must address issues, but *with* love. He may find that he can tell her she needs to go to hell, and as long as he walks her there and shows her some affection along the way, she may go there for him. He may need to become her alpha personality. An alpha personality does all of the following:

1. Commands respect
2. Genuinely likes her
3. Is stronger than she is
4. Puts her in a positive light

If he can do this, it will help manage the relationship with her. He must *not* become her therapist.

Most likely, she has been through hell and back. If it is not possible for him to be her alpha personality, and he needs to disconnect and leave the relationship, he should do it with love. She may threaten him with terrible things like an adolescent girl might do. Can she be dangerous? Yes. May she become suicidal? Yes. She probably will not carry out the suicide threats, unless she has an accident or she is under the influence of substances. He should call the authorities if she becomes dangerous to him or to herself. She may be safer in jail or in a psychiatric ward. Again, he should do it in the most loving way he can. She is desperate.

Is any of this his fault? I am sure she will think so and perhaps make up convincing scenarios about how it is his fault. However, before he accepts blame, he should answer these questions:

- Did he make her the way she is?
- Should he take her reactions personally, or would she act this way no matter who she was with?
- Can *he* deal with her?
- Does she add to his life, or detract from it in the long term?

If he answers these questions honestly, he may find the ultimate answer. Joe DiMaggio was married to Marilyn Monroe for a short time. They split, but he managed to be her loving friend. Marilyn was a flounder. She was a sexy, warm and cold, abused, and privileged human being. She could be one's greatest fantasy and worst nightmare. She felt lonely, even with all her admirers. She felt empty, even with all her fame and accomplishments. She was a girl inside a full-grown woman's body.

I have been a psychologist for a long time, and most therapists will tell you this: you can't change anyone. He is not going to be her savior. He is not going to change her. He can change only himself and his relationship with her.

What's more, the only good changes are the changes that change people *back*. We are perfectly fine when we come into this world. We are perfect little babies . . . and then things happen that change us, like trauma and invalidation. So you see, *change* is actually the problem. Don't mistake change with development or transformation, which is becoming *more* of who you are. In a way, trauma changes who a person *is*. Invalidation and abuse make people hide their real selves, shamefully. Neglect changes people. See what I mean? The problem is that she has changed. He should not try to put a good change on top of a bad change. It is better to take away the bad change or fix the bad change, and that should be left up to her therapist.

The Blowfish (Ms. Bullee)

In elementary school, girls tend to bully differently from the ways boys do. Boys will use physical force, and then by high school, it turns into verbal abuse. Girls bully by "outcasting" another girl and by using emotional abuse. "Outcasting" is when a girl or woman gets everyone else to stop associating with the victim. The blowfish may invite all the girls except the victim to a birthday party. There have been several TV shows about girls bullying other girls. I was on the Montel Williams show with parents whose daughter had committed suicide because she was being shunned, ridiculed, and threatened by her peers. Teenagers (boys as well as girls) go through a phase during which their peers' opinions about them are even more important than the opinions of their parents. On the show, there were several girls from the school who participated in the outcasting of the suicide victim. They described how they had degraded her and called her names to the point that she felt her life wasn't worth living. Because death is not real to most teenagers, they never expected her to commit suicide—it never entered their minds.

Some women do the same thing. They don't outgrow it. They are just more subtle about it and more "professional." A woman who was a supervisor attended a seminar. It was meant to be a basic seminar, and if she had read the brochure, she would have realized it. This woman hastily made her employees take the course with her. These people were beyond a basic seminar and didn't get much out of it. Instead of admitting she had made a mistake and requesting her money back for everyone, she resorted to undermining the seminar and blaming the seminar leader. At lunch she spoke to several people about the seminar and how lousy it was. Normally, people enjoyed the seminar. After lunch there was an extreme drop in morale. She came back from lunch with a negative attitude that filled the room, and she asked advanced questions. The instructor declined to answer because the questions were above the knowledge that most people had in the seminar, and the instructor didn't want to confuse them. During the seminar, the supervisor was constantly talking to others and making faces. She had outcasted the instructor to as many people as she could. The instructor should have politely asked her to leave. She was a very educated professional but was still using the outcasting to deal with things.

To a girl, outcasting is very intimidating. Women and girls who use this "technique" are trying to win and be "right." If they get everyone else's support, it justifies their actions and covers up their own insecurities about themselves. Outcasting is unproductive and unnecessary, but maybe that's all the person knows how to do. In families where it's important to be "right" and "win," it becomes a matter of dominance. In other words, the dominant one is the one who is "right." It is usually the mother or father who is the example, always winning and being right. The offspring adopt this dysfunctional way of dealing with things, and it supersedes fairness and empathy in interactions with others. In these families, if one makes a mistake or does not perform well, he or she gets degraded and invalidated instead of being corrected or given suggestions for improvement. As adults, they are not trying to be mean and nasty but are just dealing with things as they have been taught.

Some women (and men) use outcasting when they are upset with their spouse. They let the children know what a jerk the spouse is. They may not realize the damage this causes to the children. Children can make up their own minds (if not now, then eventually). It is not good for a child to think badly of a parent (sometimes even if that parent has big faults). They will see the faults when they are ready and can handle it. It is very damaging to alienate a child from a parent. Research shows that in a divorce situation, children are mostly affected by the conflict of the parents rather than the divorce itself. That is why most divorce agreements have a clause about not alienating the children from the other parent. Of course, some parents have such hate, bitterness, and animosity for the partner (or ex-partner) that they can't see the bigger picture and what it is doing to the children. Still other parents think they have only the children to talk to. I say, they should find someone to talk to other than their children about this. The nonverbal put-downs are just as negatively effective as the verbal invalidations. It is very difficult to contain oneself, sometimes, when splitting up. An ex-spouse may want to bully the ex just as the ex bullied him or her, but each must be careful of the little eyes and ears watching and listening. Children learn from example even more than from what is said.

Bullying is all about dominance and position. The bully may be smart enough to convincingly blame the victim, but it is the mentality of the bully that rises to the surface (i.e., bullies always blame someone else and need a scapegoat). People who come from more functional families get taken off guard and may not understand the dominance mentality. They may not realize what is going on, especially if the dominating personality is good at rationalizing and blaming. But in back of all that smoke screen, it is about dominance.

In the world of dogs, one dog will act aggressively to another and the second dog may show submission by lying on the ground and showing its neck. Then the first dog may not feel threatened. Unfortunately, some humans are still that primitive. However, it may be necessary to be that primitive, depending on who is being dealt with. In dealing with some personalities, it is going to be they or you who submits. On the Montel Williams show, the leader of the pack did not show up. The girls who "submitted" to this leader appeared and were remorseful about what they had done. They all said that they were just trying to stay on the good side of the leader. By saying this, they weren't trying to blame the leader. They were just trying to take responsibility for their part in it and tell the truth about the situation. I can imagine the leader blaming the victim for taking her own life, justifying what she did, and being fearful about what might happen to herself if everyone blamed her for what happened. These kinds of leaders don't usually get fearful about things, except what might happen to them personally if they are found out.

So that's the game. What does a man dealing with this personality do? Either submit or dominate. If he thinks this person is going to be a fair leader, then he may submit. If he can see that he isn't going to be able to work with the bully, then he should dominate or leave her presence. There is one other possible alternative: mutual respect. That's where each party knows where the other is coming from and they are going to try to work together. He will not try to dominate her. He won't allow her to dominate. He will do the following:

1. Demand respect.
2. Give respect.
3. Show that he likes the bully (if that is possible).
4. Put the bully in a good light.

The blowfish needs to sense that he respects her and will not be dominated. If she senses it, she will end up treating him differently than she treats those whom she can dominate. She may be a little on guard that he may try to dominate her, but she is comfortable with him because he likes her. A bully needs and responds well to nurturing. He should never give nurturing to her in a condescending way and should never look down upon her. He should just find reasons to like her, admire her (genuinely), and support her. If he can't do that, he should watch out!

I remember a time when I had gone to the Philippines for three weeks. I couldn't understand the language, so I learned to read people and understand people nonverbally by seeing their expressions and actions. I was accustomed to being in this mode when I returned to the United States and attended an executive meeting in White Plains. These executives were getting together for the first time. What I saw, nonverbally, made me chuckle. There were several executives jockeying for position. Who was going to be the leader of the leaders? One by one, they were submitting and "showing their necks" (e.g., looking down, looking away, becoming quiet, smiling a pretend smile, saying "OK"). It came down to the final two. Who was going to be the winner? Finally, one executive did the equivalent of lifting his leg and urinating on the other, and that was the determining factor. It was like a pack of dogs, in a way. And it isn't the most rational one or the fairest one who wins. It is the most dominant one. Perhaps the one with the biggest mouth (scariest growl) wins. This usually ends up correcting itself, because if the dominant one turns out to be unfair or irrational, the leaders who have mutual respect for each other end up getting together and ousting the defective dominant one.

Although bullies may use different tactics and look for different ends, the basic core motivations are the same: dominance and competition. The bottom line for some people is not about fairness, ethics, or the greater good. It's about dominance. It helps to know the game that is being played when you see it going on.

In bullies (male or female) one will see the trilogy: ego, arrogance, and sense of entitlement. It's like a cat that is confronting an enemy. Ever see the fur go up and the cat curl its back up high so it looks bigger? A cat will even stand on its hind legs to look bigger and let out an awful-sounding groan.

We had a cat that was really kind of a wimp, but he was big. We lived in a townhouse and the man next door had two black Labradors. They were big but young and still had the mentality of puppies. They would come to our back patio door sometimes. If our cat saw them, he would get all angry, raise his fur, let out a deep groan, and run across the kitchen floor lickety-split. He would get to the patio door and pound it with his paws making a "boom-boom" sound vibrating on the glass and scaring the dogs away. Then he would stick his butt up in the air and pompously walk away like he was the king of the jungle. Well, one summer day I had the patio door open and one of my children had opened the screen and forgotten to close it. I was engrossed in some work at the kitchen table, and the dogs had come to the door. The cat happened to walk into the kitchen and see the dogs, and he went into his usual tirade with the fur standing up, the kitty roar, and the mad dash to the patio door. He stood up on his hind legs when he reached the patio doorway and went to boom-boom the glass . . . but it wasn't there and he ended up flying outside with the dogs. He froze in his tracks on the patio. The dogs were licking his frozen self, and you could see his wet fur standing up on his head where the dogs licked him. He was totally shocked. Ever so cautiously he moved away from the dogs and back into the kitchen. Then he turned and trotted away, looking back a couple of times with a humiliated expression on his face. He shot me a glance as he turned the corner, and he looked totally humiliated. I laughed so hard I almost fell out of the chair.

Ego is like a balloon. One little prick and it noisily disappears. With a good self-esteem, a little prick is just a little prick. I realized I had seen this before with some executives. I remember a very charismatic woman who became vice president. So many times I would hear an executive manager say something like, "I am going to put her in her place. She is going to get a reality adjustment." She was so good at maintaining her position that the manager would end up falling on his own sword. She would facilitate him in making himself look as bad as he was. She had the respect of her managers (vs. operating on fear). She was self-assured (vs. egotistical), confident (vs. arrogant), purposeful (vs. entitled), and passionate (vs. angry). She was inquisitive instead of defensive. She was caring about people without being condescending or acting like a mother. She wasn't dominating so much as she would not and could not be dominated. She didn't get involved with that game. She had true charisma and *that* is what made her a leader. It wasn't the tricks she knew, or the psychological games, or the dominance techniques, it was *who* she was that counted. She wasn't going to be bullied. Men tend to identify with *what* they are and *what* they do. Women tend to gravitate to a "beingness" rather than a "doingness" in their style. It can work very well. Are you *who* you could be? I don't mean to suggest that we change our personality, just take it to the next level. We will see more about this in the section "The Universal Resolution." (Don't peek ahead, though. This book is a process, not a bunch of end products.)

The Piranha (Ms. Bullee-Tootoo)

I don't have much to say about the piranha. She goes along with the bully so she doesn't get attacked. She takes out her frustrations by helping the bully gang up on someone else.

She is a follower, like a chicken. In the barnyard, some hens can look threatening. They look at others with their beaks pointed in another's direction and walks toward that individual in a threatening way along with the other chickens. All someone has to do is wave his arms and shout "Boo" and she flees, squawking all the way. She isn't very deep and she doesn't see the bigger picture. Her purpose is self-preservation, which is all there is to say about her.

The Shark (Ms. Eetcha)
The shark has a disregard for the feelings and plight of others, although she can pretend to be concerned. She lacks a conscience. She has ego, arrogance, and a sense of entitlement. She appears to think well of herself. She appears to be confident, and she feels entitled. She does not come off as being neurotic or having any worries. She can be very gregarious and fun-loving. She knows what she wants at any given moment but usually lacks larger goals, except to state some just for effect. And she doesn't follow through to earn her goals. After all, she is "entitled." She doesn't mind breaking the rules for her own gain. She can be very manipulative, aggressive, and pushy, if she has to be. Otherwise, she may be very charming and talk a man or woman into giving her the shirt off his or her back. She may promise to give him or her something in return, but it won't happen. In fact, she loses respect for him when he succumbs to her manipulation, secretly thinking he is a loser for falling for her con job.

This one is bad news. He should stay away. He has nothing to gain and everything to lose by relating with her. There is only one important person in the world to the shark, and that is herself. Another person is only as important as what he can contribute to her well-being. When he is no longer valuable to her, he is a zero. She will have no compassion and no sympathy for him, although she can pretend to be compassionate and sympathetic if she is not done using him yet.

She accomplishes her goals with manipulation or force. She believes that only the strong survive and sees herself as the primary survivor. She misinterprets kindness for weakness. She believes in a dog-eat-dog world; she has to get him first before he gets her. She is always lying and cheating and feels nothing about it, unless she gets caught. She feels unfairly treated and is always out to get her just dues. She blames others for her own transgressions. She blames her victims. If the victim can't take care of himself, that is not her problem.

She can be very deceptive and doesn't mind breaking the law if she thinks she won't get caught. She has no qualms about getting physical if needed. She usually has debts that she doesn't pay and obligations she doesn't meet. Her children often fend for themselves. She can leave her spouse and her children with very little remorse. She can be very irritable and aggressive.

Until a person gets to know her, she can appear to be too good to be true. She loves to have fun, and he may get caught up in her reckless abandon. She seems to be so confident (arrogant); she knows what she wants and goes for it (entitlement). She may use drugs recreationally. She may be uninhibited sexually. She likes to go over the limits and boundaries.

If a man wants to be with her, he should have a good time while he can, because misery is around the next corner. If they are stopped by the police, she will put the marijuana she brought with her in his glove compartment and feign that she had no idea that he was a druggie. He should not put her name on his checking account unless he wants bounced checks. He should not give her access to family heirlooms. She is liable to take them down to the pawnshop, indifferent to the emotional value of the items. If he confronts her with taking the items, she may deny it, saying a burglar must have done it. If he catches her red-handed, she may say, "Oh come on. What was I supposed to do? I needed a couple of dollars. If you loved me like you say, you would give me what I need and then I wouldn't have to do these things," implying that her transgressions are his fault.

Why is she this way? Theorists say it is a genetic temperament in combination with environmental conditions. Sounds reasonable, doesn't it? I would add that it is also a series of choices. When the conscience interferes with what the individual wants, it makes her "weak" so she actively works toward eliminating this "weakness." From my work in forensics, I have developed a firm belief that there is a big difference between mental illness and criminality. There are plenty of schizophrenics that wouldn't hurt a flea, despite their hallucinations. Then there are schizophrenics who nurture a criminal nature, and their criminality has little to do with their mental illness. The shark's temperament can be nurtured on the dark side and become self-serving. The shark is a criminal. Some people think that people who do bad things just have problems. Nope. There really is such a thing as evil. The person who is evil does not necessarily have to do things that instigate evil. She just has to do things that disregard the rights of others for her own self-gain. Like I said, this person might not deliberately want to hurt someone *just* to hurt him, but if he gets in the way of her dinner, it will be necessary for her to get rid of him. Then she will say, "I really liked him. He was a nice guy. But I had to take care of myself."

What can he do about it? Get out of her life. That is the solution—no *if*, *and*, or *but*. Do I make myself clear? He should not worry about her. She will be OK. She will find another sucker. Am I saying this with animosity? No, actually, it is just the objective answer, based on the research and all the information of therapists, psychologists, and counselors who have exhausted their energies and failed at rehabilitating someone like this.

If he is not going to heed my suggestion and has decided he is going to hang out with this person anyway, there are only a few things he can do to manage her.

1. Demand respect from her.
2. Show admiration. (She responds to admiration and not necessarily love, because she sees love as a weakness.)

3. Never ask for mercy (that just turns her on like a cat playing with a mouse).
4. Hold her in a good light to others.
5. Be more powerful than she is. (Of course, the minute he loses his power, she will eat him up.)

We are dealing with a predator here. If he wanted to have a lioness as his pet, think of what he would have to do. Treat her with respect, demand respect, be nice to her but don't give in, be in command of her, and never, never stand between her and her next meal.

If a man works for her, he should be advised that she will use him. She will make any promises he wants to hear. Then after he works hard and helps her to achieve that promotion, she could move on to the next level and forget all about him, unless he can be of further use to her.

The Bottom Dweller (Ms. O. B. Livious)

Ms. O. B. Livious may come from a couple of different psychological origins. She hangs out with losers. No matter what her psychological origin is, she has a self-esteem problem.

Examples:

• **Type I.** She feels superior when she hangs out with low-lifers. She has an esteem problem. It may be that she would rather be the queen of the low-lifers than just another suburbanite. She may prefer to be a big fish in a small pond instead of the same-size fish in a bigger pond.

Her reign of superiority may last for a time, but she may find she is not as street-smart as her subjects. She eventually falls from grace, and they find a new victim to crown. It happens so subtly that she never sees it coming.

- **Type II.** She may go on a crusade to save people. She sees the potential in people, and she is idealistic. She crosses boundaries and makes her crusade a part of her personal life instead of a line of work or a volunteer job. If a nice-looking man comes along who has a lot of potential but can't seem to get it together, she marries him. She is a savior. She is gallant, noble, and doesn't see the realistic big picture of things. Twenty years later, her husband still hasn't got it together and she is burned out. Her esteem is in great jeopardy when she starts to realize that she failed. She is a giver who needs a taker to make her feel good about herself.
- **Type III.** She has very little prefrontal lobe activity. She doesn't know who she is. She doesn't see the big picture of things. She is shocked when her drug-dealing boyfriend has sex with her best friend. Her boyfriend beat her up, but that was because she was talking to a guy and smiling at him. All she has to do is not smile at any guy and things will be OK from now on. Her friends have told her not to do cocaine because it can be addictive. Her boyfriend told her it wasn't addictive. "Hell," he said, "I have been doing it every day for five years, and I'm not addicted." She can be beautiful, nice, and even intellectually smart, but she has no common sense and no view of the big picture. She is not yet awake in some ways. There are dead bodies of

people who have tried to help her along the path of her life. You could be next.

It is not that the bottom dweller is overtly nasty. She seems just the opposite. But she will drain the energy and resources of those who try to help her. They keep knocking on her mind's door, but no one is home. The lights are on, but the house is empty. A mind is a terrible thing to waste, but she hasn't located hers yet. She is a victim. Perhaps she is a well-dressed, beautiful, and intellectual victim with a lot of potential, but she is a victim nonetheless. If someone still wants to help her, maybe he should read "Type II." If he would like to run off with her and take her away from all that, maybe he should read "Type II" again.

No. He can be her friend if he wishes, but he must not have great expectations of her enlightenment. He should not save her butt by marrying her or riding away with her on his white horse. I know it's tempting. It looks like she is "almost there." A little boost from him and she may get it together, in which case she would be eternally grateful to him for helping her see the light. He should get a life! *He* has an esteem problem. He should go find someone he doesn't have to fix. What's the matter?! He thinks he's not good enough? He should go see a therapist.

If he does run off with her and take her away from all that, what he may find twenty years from now is that she is still "almost there." And he has marks all over his body where he threw himself in the path of her life. He ends up resenting her, but he can't blame her because she doesn't know any better. All he has done is transformed her from Ms. O. B. Livious to Mrs. O. B. Livious.

The Surface Dweller (Ms. Skimmy)

At first she may seem colorful, sexy, entertaining, impressive, engaging, and exciting. She is seductive and provocative. Her clothes are the latest and the best. She treats a man as if she has known him for years. He may feel quickly connected to her. She is personable. She seems to like him right away. He might feel like he could take advantage of her if he really wanted to. She is kind of gullible. She loves the attention he gives her.

After he gets to know her, he finds that her emotions are not deep and they can change rapidly. She has to be the center of attention. If he doesn't give the attention to her, she will get it somewhere else. She takes great care in her physical appearance. She is flirtatious and demanding and can be ruthless. She may have difficulty with spending, eating, and sexing. She is uninterested in empathizing with others except in a dramatic, superficial way.

She doesn't believe that others deserve the attention, wealth, fame, or recognition they get. She actually feels inadequate but hides it with an illusion of high self-worth and ego. She actually feels insecure and weak and overcompensates for those feelings by exaggerating and building herself up to others. She is looking for the ideal mate to affirm and confirm her status. She is high-maintenance and expects him to conform to her wishes. She wants things that she doesn't earn, and she tries to impress people she doesn't like.

If he starts sinking or doesn't give her the attention she needs, she is off to see someone who has the status and will give her the attention she feels she deserves. She likes to be supported in the custom she believes she is entitled to (that would be unlimited resources and unlimited attention). This can be exhausting (emotionally and financially) for him. She may turn into a philanthropist with his money and give it away until he is broke. Then she may turn on him and leave him because he obviously is not as wealthy as he said. He must have deceived her. What a loser he must be, she thinks. Anyway, he couldn't be her soul mate. It's time to look for someone who appreciates her more than he does. As he is going bankrupt, she may dramatically feign some sympathy his way, as she introduces him to her new (more successful) paramour.

This may go on until she falls flat on her face (if she ever does). She is going to need a significant event in her life (life-threatening incident, loss of a significant other, etc.) to change her. Only after she falls is there a chance of change. She is then prone to shame and humiliation. She may become a hypochondriac trying to illicit sympathy (which she was so stingy about giving). She may have self-contempt for her failure to secure the fantasy she desperately wanted for herself. She takes offense at the smallest hint of judgment from others. Her feelings of excitement have turned to emptiness.

At that point, he should *not* try to enable her ego. Instead, he should find the genuine attributes that she has and acknowledge her for them. Her thinking is skewed because she has been trying to make up for her perceived inadequacies with good looks and grandiose expectations of herself and others. At this vulnerable point, she needs to know that she is appreciated for who she is (underneath the veneer). That is where her problem started to begin with. She was led to believe that who she is was less important than what she has. Most likely, she came from a dysfunctional family where the value was not in the person but in the superficial circumstance surrounding the person. Hence, the feeling of insecurity and inadequacy, and the desperate attempt to fill in these holes with success, accomplishment, and good looks. That is also why she may have trouble with overeating, spending, and other addictions. She is trying to fill in the emptiness she feels, but she can do so only temporarily. She is so narcissistic because she could never pass through that stage in her development because she didn't have the unconditional love from her family of origin.

She is not a devil, just dysfunctional. But he should be careful, she can still hurt him no matter how much love he has to give her and no matter how much he cares. He should not throw himself on the train tracks of her life. There are probably already people on those tracks who have been run over trying to help her. She may be too proud to accept help and may never admit she needs it.

There are many family programs across the country that she may be able to attend on a full-day basis (e.g., at this writing, The Caron Foundation in Wernersville, Pennsylvania; The Meadows near Phoenix, Arizona; and Sierra Tucson near Tucson, Arizona). Group therapy helps, as does individual counseling with a therapist who is familiar with her plight and who has had success with her kind of problems.

What can someone do? Nurture her, but do not reward her ego, arrogance, or entitlement.

The Octopus (Ms. Doña Juanita)

She genuinely loves the male species. Why shouldn't she? Men provide her with things, material and immaterial. She is a master at stroking and pricking the jujube doll. She is with yet another guy, but this time, this is really "the one" (like the other twelve guys before him). She can manipulate the biggest and smallest egos. She puts men to the test. If they pass her test, she loses respect for them for allowing her to manipulate them. If they fail the test, they are of no use to her anyway. She surrounds herself with men who heed her beck and call. She becomes whatever she needs to be in order to gain a heavy controlling presence with a man. Most men like to be controlled by her without realizing what she is doing. She stings them first with an anesthetizer (building their ego, pretending to be crazy about them, and so forth). Most anesthetics are hypnotics. They do just what she wants.

Yoda would say, "A chameleon, she is." She may be so accustomed to changing her color (changing who she is) to manipulate a man that she has forgotten her original color and no longer knows who she is. She is similar to the eel except that she would never want to be dependent on a man. She has ulterior motives, not dependency issues.

She may use a man for her pleasure or to help her bouts of loneliness, but she longs for "the one" who she is sure is going to come along anytime now. Even if she is married, she holds back that last little bit, waiting for her true prince. She has had occasions when she is sure the prince has arrived, only to be disappointed when she starts seeing the warts on his froggy self. She idealizes the prince and has expectations for the prince that no earthly man could live up to. She is a binger on men. A man comes along who might be the prince and she binges on him. She is like a binge alcoholic. A binge alcoholic doesn't drink every day, but when she does, she really ties one on. Then there is always the hangover (the wart period). That is followed by the abandonment period when she drops him like a lead balloon—whoops, sorry honey, you are not the prince. She usually has some nice tactful release excuses in her bag of tricks. Men like to "understand" why, and she accommodates them. Of course, they don't realize that "understanding" is the booby prize. It's like W. C. Fields once said: "First prize is one week in Philadelphia. Second prize is two weeks in Philadelphia." She understands this logic.

She can even remain friends with some of her ex-lovers and keep them motivated as wanna-bes. She has such charisma that she can tell a man he needs to go to hell for her in such a way that he can't wait for the trip. She is not trying to be nasty, because she does have such affection for men, but she can do a lot of damage. She may ruin marriages without taking any blame for it. The victim takes the blame along with the associated guilt and angst that go with it.

She has an illusion of love. In fact, she always falls in love with the illusion. An illusion is not a hallucination. With a hallucination, there is nothing there. With an illusion, there is something there, but the illusion obscures the actual thing itself. Her illusion keeps surrounding each man, one by one. When the illusion dissipates, she is left with a real earthly man, not a prince. When the sporty-looking car turns out to be a four cylinder and she finds out the tux was rented, she makes him disappear, like Cinderella's coach and driver at midnight.

She is idealistic. She buys into Hollywood's romantic portrayals. She thinks the excitement of a new relationship should last for the next fifty years. It's racy, but not meaningful. She thinks that her soul mate is going to complete her. In the research I have done on soul mates, the consensus is that a soul mate does not complete a person. It seems that people must be complete as individuals *first*. Then, and only then, are they ready for their soul mate. The paradox is that once they do not *need* a soul mate, he or she shows up. It's not about finding or searching. It's about being ready. Loving someone because you *need* him or her is different from loving someone because you *want* him or her. (See the description of Ms. Eel, coming up.)

What can a man do? She is not in love with him. She is in love with the illusion she has. Her illusion just happens to be hovering around him . . . for now. As soon as the fog lifts, he is going to be standing there as his earthly self, and that won't be good enough for her. She is going to hold back that last little bit, then. If he thinks she is his soul mate, he should consider the following:

1. Did he have moments with her that he felt were "perfect" and he felt high? He could be a love addict just like she is and should sign up for SLAA (Sex and Love Addicts Anonymous). No, I am not kidding. He should read Patrick Carnes's book *Out of the Shadows* and leave it lying around for her. Maybe she will pick it up.

2. After reading number 1, did he immediately think to himself that I might not know what I am talking about? I have interacted with thousands of other therapists. Is he still going to discount what I just said? If so, he should go back to number 1.

3. If he is at this point and still doesn't buy it, maybe it would help to know that this advice comes directly from the experience of love addicts. If that makes a difference, he should go back and read number 1.

4. If he is here and still wants to help her, he should read *Codependent No More* by Melody Beattie.

5. If he thinks that this number 5 is going to help him . . . help her . . . and he is not going to do what was suggested in 1, 2, 3, or 4, he is probably hopeless at this time.

He should wait until he crashes and then come back and pick up this book again. He should make sure he puts it in a place where he can find it. He will need it.

6. If he thinks this has been no help at all, because it isn't what he wanted to hear, then he should do it *his* way. Follow that yellow brick road, and he will wish he was back in Kansas.

The Eel (Ms. Dependent)

The eel feels she needs someone around her at all times. She feels helpless on her own. If her mate is not there, she may turn to someone else, only out of a perceived desperation, not because she wants to have an illicit affair. In fact, she will be scared that she will offend her primary supporter. She feels she has to do whatever he (her caretaker) says to keep his support. The worst that could happen in her perception is that she would be abandoned. That alone may actually keep her from having an affair. It's not that she loves her mate so much as she *needs* him. She feels weak and incompetent by herself. She consults him for every decision. She wants him to tell her what to do.

He may have fallen for her, initially, because it seemed that she put him on a pedestal and couldn't live without him. She would go along with everything he wanted to do. She would be happy to go hunting with him or play pool. She even learned to play pool well, so as not to offend him. She asks him about and includes him in everything she does. She seemed to be his sidekick, lover, and friend. She tells him that he is a great lover, even though other women may have had complaints. She seems too good to be true. And you know what? She *is* too good to be true.

After a time, he starts realizing some things. She starts becoming more like a burden. She wants to go with him everywhere, suffocating him. When he gets angry with her, she gives in. She doesn't seem to have any of her own opinions. When he asks her for her opinion, she will give what she thinks he wants to hear. He can never go on a business trip without taking her along. It isn't love she feels for him, it is desperation. She starts sucking him dry, but she doesn't mean to if it gets him upset. She will not protest so much if he drinks a lot. Maybe he wants her to confront him on his bad behavior because he knows he is out of control. Forget it. She won't complain. She may just cry. If he has any addictions, she will enable him to death (literally).

She will try to be the good wife (according to what she thinks he thinks a good wife should be). It is not an inherent self-motivated desire. Nothing is a self-motivated desire. It's all about her mate and what he wants. She will do unpleasant things for him to try to maintain his support. She will accommodate unpleasant and disgusting tasks. Does she enjoy it? No, but she will pretend to if it pleases him. Her gut may twist and she may get nauseated. If this is what he wished for, he got his wish.

Sometimes things are not what they seem.

She is gullible. She trusts others completely. It is a blind trust, which is not based on good judgment. She is easily taken advantage of. He may lose respect for her and leave her. If he does, she may jump right into a relationship with someone else. She didn't think he was so terrific after all. She was just using him to get by. Someone else can easily replace him. It wasn't about love, it was about dependency.

What can he do if he wants to stay with her and help her? He can use her motivation to please him by trying to get her to do things that she wants to do (if he can ever find out what those things may be). He will need other relationships (not romantic relationships) with people who can call him on his stuff (who are not afraid to tell him when he is doing something inappropriate). He will need to use her dependency needs to do the best for *her*. If he does this, maybe she can be happy, and maybe she will learn to look up to him as a good human being instead of just an authority figure. He will have to create a paradox where a dependent person who wants "to please" can please him by being an independent person and *not* always pleasing him.

The Sponge (Ms. Codependent)

She absorbs the pain and shelters her significant other and her children from reality. What an angel she seems to be. She makes excuses for her mate after he ties one on. She calls in sick for him at work. She protects the children from knowing that he is a fall-down-drunk. (P.S. They know.) If she can just get him to function enough to keep his job. Whoops! He got fired. It's time for her to get a job. She gets a job and still does the wash, does the dishes, and makes sure the kids are off to school. She gets frustrated sometimes, but his verbal abuse usually quiets her down enough for her to "keep peace" in the family. She tries to "help" him by pouring the booze down the sink, but when he gets angry at her, she gives him money and he disappears for the evening. She tries hard to keep up pretenses, telling everyone, "He is looking for a job but there is no work to be found."

She is an angel, all right. An angel of death. She doesn't realize it, of course, but she is enabling her husband right into the grave. Not that she caused his alcoholism, but she is helping him with his addiction. She is the "good cop." He may never recover from alcoholism, but with her around, it is a guarantee. Oh, she hates the drinking and is totally against it. She lets him know from time to time after her resentment builds so much she can't stand it. Maybe he will hit her then and say he is sorry the next day.

If he reforms, she won't know what to do. She may take up with another budding alcoholic. It's not that she wants to. Maybe her dad was an alcoholic. She knows how to deal with alcoholism, but if that is not an issue, she may feel lost. Being a sponge is familiar to her. She knows how to absorb the pain and shame of others' dysfunctions. Unwittingly, she creates the atmosphere for relapse. "You haven't had a drink for two weeks, honey. Go ahead and have a beer. Just one though, OK?"

Right!

Life without turmoil is difficult for her. She is dependent on her husband and his addiction, or rather . . . codependent. If her husband stops drinking, maybe the daughter will start. She has to have some turmoil in her life from somewhere.

If you want to be her friend, what can be done to help her? Invite her to an Al-Anon meeting. It's an anonymous group of people who are connected to alcoholics. Give her *Codependent No More* to read. There is excellent help out there now for this mentality.

She has to make the decision: "It's me or the alcohol." She has to be willing to pull the rug out from underneath her addicted significant other. She can't change him, but she can change herself and change the relationship. She has to kick the caterpillar out the door. If the caterpillar comes back as a butterfly, it can be good. If not, it wasn't meant to be. He will have to destroy himself without her help then. At least she won't be an angel of death.

I know this sounds simple, but I also know it is very hard. Yet, it needs to be done for her sake and the sake of the alcoholic. She may love him, but sooner or later, one way or the other, it is going to be a choice between her and the alcohol, anyway. It is better to make the decision now rather than wait for chronic alcoholism to set in with all its related health problems and dysfunctional family problems.

The Corporate Bullhead (Ms. Anal-izer)

She is perfectionistic, rigid, moralistic, formal, distant, competitive, intellectual, impatient, controlled, controlling, inflexible, and stubborn. She may hoard things as would a pack rat, wanting to keep every piece of paper. She is a workaholic in excess of normal workaholics. She may be preoccupied with neatness and orderliness. She may have a tendency to do things herself because she believes no one else can do them as thoroughly as she can. She tends to get so involved in the details that she loses sight of the bigger picture. There seem to be so many details that she feels overwhelmed and overburdened. She blames part of this on her staff members who she thinks are frivolous and have no sense of responsibility. She is especially covertly hostile to those who show emotions or seem to be impulsive.

She values integrity, discipline, order, and loyalty. She loathes anyone who doesn't have a responsible work ethic, which includes loathing everyone to some degree because no one could be perfect enough to live up to her expectations (including herself). Being very stoic herself, she doesn't think others have a right to be angry. She does everything according to the rules. She is not much fun to work with or to work for. She doesn't have much of a sense of humor.

She has to be in control of her relationships. She is usually the dominant one. Although she doesn't get physical, her tongue can be poisonous at home and in the workplace if things seem out of control. She insists on conformity and is authoritarian in her relationships at home and the office. Her husband and children can never live up to her expectations. She is rarely pleased.

At the office, she is condescending to her employees but very ingratiating to her superiors. She gives them what they want, and if she can't she blames her employees for being the irresponsible, ungrateful, disloyal people she believes they are. Despite her feelings, she is cordial and formal to her subordinates. She has a hard time understanding why she has a morale problem.

She has trouble performing well in environments that require anything more than strict guidelines and rules. Despite the overtime she puts in, she doesn't get a whole lot of work done. Her attentiveness to meaningless details supersedes her understanding of the bigger picture.

She hardly ever takes a vacation, but when she does, it is filled with details of places to visit and a time schedule to make sure she gets all the vacationing done.

As a child, she was probably punished for failure and hardly rewarded for success. Life was serious. There was no time for fun. She may tend to neglect her family for work, and her children may look forward to her absence.

Unless she has a nervous breakdown before middle age, she may come in for therapy at that time because she is looking for help to increase her productivity at work. Her memory is not as good as it once was, and she can't seem to handle the workload like she used to. The therapist is probably going to notice a depression. An antidepressant is probably not going to help this person because the depression originates from a psychological perspective rather than a physiological depression. The serotonin vitamins (Prozac, Paxil, Zoloft, etc.) are not going to help much, and it is doubtful whether she would take them anyway, out of a fear of losing control. Her problem is usually that her inner child has gone to sleep from boredom and she doesn't allow herself to rejuvenate her inner child through activities that give her life meaning. Meaning to her is duty and responsibility.

Her drugs of choice are legal drugs. She may use alcohol, Xanax, or Ativan to calm down. She may use uppers (prescribed, of course) to stimulate her to accomplish her work.

She has diminished prefrontal lobe activity. The prefrontal lobe is that part of the brain that enables a human being to see the bigger picture of things. It is the captain's station on the life-ship surrounded by windows, where humans can see where they have been, where they are going, and 360 degrees around them in a complete circle. She hardly sits in the captain's station. She is too busy running around the ship, making sure that her crew is doing its job . . . correctly. If someone tells her exactly where the ship is supposed to go, she will draw out the most detailed navigation plan. If someone tells her to go "someplace nice," it stops her in her tracks.

Those who work for her and try to keep up with her probably won't succeed. She breathes and sleeps work and responsibility. Even if they do keep up with her, they will get criticized the same way she criticizes herself. They should not look to her for any kind of acknowledgment. If she gives a raise or promotion, it will be because the guidelines say that it's time.

For a spouse or offspring, it is the same. She has a lot of expectations that are unrealistic. If they happen to meet one of her unrealistic expectations, then things have gone the way she expected they should. There will be no reward, but there will be punishment for not meeting her other expectations. It is close to impossible to make her happy. Happiness and joy are frivolous.

Her students should be advised that she is going to take heavy points off for spelling and for not having a report typed. It doesn't matter how much the student has done or how brilliant the report is. She is incapable, most of the time, of seeing past the details to the bigger picture. She was able to get through school by having the capacity to remember the details. She is not going to appreciate creativity.

The most therapeutic management for a student, family member, or employee of the corporate bullhead would be to be kind to her, to not take her criticisms personally, and to avoid her. They would probably be happier that way. It may be easy to do that because she will be consumed with details and work most of the time, anyway. She is probably not trying to be nasty. She is just preoccupied inside her own private psychological prison cell.

WHAT TO DO

You've got to know when to hold 'em,
know when to fold 'em.
—KENNY ROGERS, "THE GAMBLER"

I have already given you suggestions on how to deal with specific types of nasty women. Now it's time for the big stuff. Did I forget to give you special "lines" or "tricks"? No, I didn't forget. You're just not going to get any—kidding! I'll give you a few at the end that seem to work in most situations. I give you these to tide you over until you *process* yourself up to the level where you don't need them. The key to dealing with nasty women is to understand them, and thereby develop yourself. It's an ongoing process, not an end product. The process is what I am going to show you first.

Understand Others

If you wanted to learn how to play baseball, would the coach just show you a bunch of strategies? That wouldn't do. To truly teach you baseball, the coach would first help you to understand the game and the positions of the players and their roles. The coach might tell you that the pitcher on the other team will be trying to make you fail. It isn't personal. That's just the role he or she plays. I interviewed a baseball player from the Phillies on my show, and he said that if you want to be a baseball player, you have to learn to handle failure. He said that you are going to fail to hit the ball most of the time. If you hit one ball out of ten, you may be a good player. Don't worry. We are going to shoot for nine out of ten.

The coach would also tell you that you had to have practice—lots of practice. Start finding some nasty women to practice with. You will get better and better, and sometimes you will get discouraged. But if you just want quick fixes and tricks and you don't want to *understand* women, get out of my book.

Brain Functions

There are four functions of the brain that are essential in understanding women (and other human beings):

1. **The mammalian processor** has evolved over millions of years. This function is located toward the back of your skull. The mammal can record memories as far back as the

fetus, but it is not very bright. It cannot form full sentences and right now your mammal is moving its eyes across the page so you can read it, but it has no idea what I am saying. It records experiential memories, including the fifty-seven perceptions associated with each memory. It also records trauma. It is not an it, but a he or a she. I am going to address the mammal as "she" in this book. The mammal has an inherent genetic temperament. She could have a collie temperament, a German shepherd temperament, a pit bull temperament, a foo-foo (e.g., shih tzu) temperament, or any other temperament (in the human species). If you abuse a collie when it is a puppy, she may shy away from people when she grows up. If you abuse a German shepherd, she may bite people when she is an adult. A pit bull may kill people when she grows up. A shih tzu will probably still love people when she grows up (and maybe become a therapist).

2. The **logic processor** of the human being is surmised to be as big as a walnut. It has evolved from (perhaps) a million years ago and contains the cognitive memories of the human being. It isn't completely developed until a human is about five years old. When the human starts calling herself "I," that is a good sign that the logic processor is developed. Some people have cognitive memories when they are three, others not until eight. You are reading this sentence right now with your logic processor.

3. The **soma (body) processor** is not important to our discussion. It makes sure the heart beats regularly and the

hormones are regulated. I mention it, only so it doesn't get mixed up with the mammal.

4. **The prefrontal lobe processor** is developed enough to use around the age of twelve. This part makes us "situationally aware." It allows us to see the big picture of things. It is the captain's seat of the mind. You can experience the prefrontal lobe capability by doing a little mental exercise. Ready? You are aware that you are reading this page, right? And . . . you are *aware* that you are aware. Feel that? That is your prefrontal lobe capability. It sees the mammal and the logic. In fact, it coordinates the mammal and the logic. Some people have access to their prefrontal lobe early (even age five). Some people have to wait until they are twelve or much later. Science has found that the prefrontal lobe keeps developing into the late thirties.

Why is this important to dealing with nasty women? Because 38 percent of the population has prefrontal lobe difficulties. Some people do not use their prefrontal lobe at all. Federal Express drops it off around the age of twelve, but some people just never open the package. These people can be very frustrating to deal with. They don't seem to see the big picture of things. They have a lack of ability to see the consequences of their actions. They live in that moment we call "now" and deal only with what is in front of them.

Most children under the age of twelve are not situationally aware. Not being aware of their particular surroundings, they do inappropriate things, like singing out loud at a funeral, talking to their friend in school while the teacher is trying to lecture, or playing loudly while their parents are on the telephone.

Thirty-eight percent of these children grow up and still do not use the prefrontal lobe, or they use it very little. Interesting, huh? Most people do have a prefrontal lobe, but you may have to lead them into theirs because they may not initiate the mental process that gets them there.

For example, I had a female boss whom we called O. B. Livious. I remember Christmas Eve one year, when I was working in the corporate world. We were at a site that had about sixty people including four managers. Around noon the other three managers told their people to go home. Our boss was working in her office, and we expected her to come out at any minute and tell us to go home. One o'clock passed. One-thirty passed. The place was quiet except for us. Finally, she walked by us and stopped to talk. One of the employees hinted, "Hey boss, what are you doing for Christmas vacation?"

She gave us a detailed description and then went back to her office. Everyone was ticked off and saying nasty things about her. They accused her of trying to bleed us for every minute she could. They thought she was letting us know who was boss, and a hundred other imaginings. Finally one person went down to her office and simply said, "Everyone else has gone home for Christmas. Do you think we could leave a bit early?"

She looked up and said immediately, "Oh! Sure!"

Then she walked down to our area and told us to go home and gave us a friendly "Merry Christmas!"

She wasn't being nasty, and she had no ulterior motives. How do people operate who don't use the prefrontal lobe? They follow rules. Their prefrontal lobe substitute is following the rules they were raised with or the rules of the corporation, church, community, and culture. They like to know the rules and feel uncomfortable when they don't.

I'll tell a couple of mammal stories now.

As I previously stated, the mammal stores memories of our traumas. She stores them in the section labeled "Danger. Volatile unconscious memories." Someone who was hit by a car may be overly cautious about crossing the road. The mammal is programmed to sense danger, and she associates the road with danger. A person may not even remember being hit by the car if it happened in early childhood, but the mammal part of her does. If she was hit by a 1955 red Chevy and her husband brings home a 1955 red Chevy, she may have a bad reaction. He thinks it is a great classic car and wants her to ride in it, and she refuses. He doesn't know why, and she doesn't know why. He may think she is mad at him for something else or she is just being difficult. She wants him to get rid of the car, even though she had previously agreed that he could buy a classic car as a hobby. Adrenaline courses through her body when she looks at the car, altering her brain chemistry and making her combative. He asks her if it is that time of the month, and she gets even more furious. He tells her she has already agreed to it and he is keeping the darn car. She doesn't feel safe with it around. It's so old. What if it catches fire and burns the house down? He thinks she is being ridiculous. Part of her thinks she *is* being ridiculous, but she still doesn't want the car around. They argue all weekend. Finally, her dad comes to visit, sees the car, and notices her reaction to it. They finally understand after he tells the story of her being hit by a car just like that one.

The husband says he is sorry for accusing her of being hormonal, rigid, going back on their agreement, and so on. She says she is sorry for overreacting. They sell the car and live happily ever after.

But usually it doesn't work that way, and a couple may never know what the real cause of their dispute is. That's where a "leap of faith" is necessary.

If she doesn't have a pattern of these types of reactions, he should not take it so personally. If he can believe in her enough that he believes she has his best interest at heart, then they can get by these things that are not understood.

Do you want more clarification? OK, let me tell another story.

A woman attending a university had three credit hours to go to get her degree. There was only one man who taught the remaining course, and most students liked him. She was also likable. The first night in class, she walked into the classroom and saw the professor. She immediately did not like him, and she sat in the back. All during the course, she was oppositional—defiant. She opposed things he said, talked to him with disrespect, and defied him whenever he gave the homework. He had to ask her to leave a couple of times because she was disrupting the class. She failed the class because she refused to do the homework he gave.

That summer, she went to see a therapist because she really needed to get through the course and didn't know how she could. Lo and behold, it came out that her uncle had molested her at the age of four, and this professor had the same glasses and the same physique as her uncle. "Ah!" she said, "Now I understand!" The therapist wanted her to stay for more sessions, but the student said she didn't have time and she was sure she would be OK now. So, do you think she was OK?

Well, she went back to the class in the fall, walked into the classroom, and saw him standing there; the mammal part of her started growling inside. Adrenaline hit her system, and she felt the same way she had felt before.

The good news is that she made it through class anyway. She did it by "blindfolding" her mammal. After that night, she walked into the class with her head down and sat in the back. She made sure she did not look at him. Luckily, his voice did not sound like her uncle's, so she was able to take notes and get through the class. Her mammal was none the wiser (it never is).

You see how this works? The weight-loss programs recommend that you don't walk down the candy aisle at the supermarket. If you do, the mammal gets triggered and you may buy some. I would also recommend that you don't *think* about candy. The mammal is not bright enough to tell the difference between fantasy and the real thing. If you fantasize about candy long enough, the mammal may start salivating, get in the car, and drive to the supermarket. Oh, you didn't know the mammal could drive? Well, you taught her to. All the while you were figuring out how to drive, you were repeating the driving behavior over and over again. Now the mammal knows how to drive. Who do you think is driving while you are talking on your cell phone? She is. It's OK though, because she can sense danger. If someone pulls over into your lane, she will gasp and you will drop your cell phone and take over.

Fascinating, isn't it?

Now try to get into your prefrontal lobe for a second because I want to sum this up with the bigger picture.

If humans react without knowing why . . . and if we are downloaded (cultured, socialized, and so forth) in the logic section with rules to operate on . . . then what part of you is seeing how it works (the big picture)? It can't be the mammal (not bright enough). It can't be the logic, if you are *seeing* the logic, so it must be the prefrontal lobe capability. Can you see yourself (imagine yourself, be aware of yourself) reading this book? All right then. If you can, you are in your prefrontal lobe.

Sometimes you don't know why you react to things the way you do, and you don't necessarily know why other people react a certain way, so before you take it personally . . . don't take it personally. *That is one of the foremost and best secrets of dealing with nasty women.*

You may remind her mammal of someone. Your glasses may remind her mammal of someone. Your car may remind her mammal of a trauma. You may look like her abusive mom or dad. You may never know why she reacts the way she does. Later in the book, I will talk about a universal technique for dealing with her.

Temperament

There are a variety of different temperaments and several scales and models to define them (e.g., The Enneagram, Myers-Briggs, Keirsey). Each tries to identify different temperaments and what affects the temperaments. Some people believe that ADHD (attention deficit/hyperactivity disorder) is a temperament that we do not honor in our society. It is called the warrior's temperament. Those with ADHD are kids and adults who get distracted by sounds and movements. If we were at war and I had to be in a foxhole with someone, I would hope to get in a foxhole with someone diagnosed with ADHD. They hear everything that makes a sound, they see everything that moves, and they may shoot first and ask questions later. I would be safe there.

I personally believe that there is a "bipolar" temperament and this temperament has great gifts. The bipolar temperament that goes awry is then called the bipolar disorder.

There are film directors and artists who are bipolar. They can be very creative, charming, fast paced, and witty. They can also get in your face and drive you crazy with attention to every detail. It's actually a requirement that a film director be bipolar (kidding!!).

My purpose here in talking about temperament is not to come up with a whole new scale on temperaments or try to identify new temperaments. There is already enough written on that. I just want to give the "feeling" of temperaments, then add in some factors that may take us to the next level of understanding.

If you visit the dog pound, you will come into contact with a lot of different temperaments. There are dogs that seem vicious and snarl at you. There are some that bark obnoxiously to get your attention. I know there are passive-aggressive dogs because I had one. These dogs are potty trained but will mess on your carpet if they are upset with you. Other dogs in the pound quietly look at you with those pathetic eyes. Others are friendly, sociable, and want to make friends. Still others have a quiet and cooperative temperament. They may not be a lot of fun, but they will be compliant. Some are very protective of their masters and will sacrifice their life to defend them. Others will try to make friends with the burglar. We pick our dogs according to the relationship we want with them.

Let's take some different temperaments and compare them. Nature needs all the different temperaments. When we are at peacetime, our jails fill up with people whom we perceive as having violent temperaments and those who don't see the consequences of what they are doing (i.e., who don't use their prefrontal lobe). In wartime, these same people who may be aggressive and totally in the moment become war heroes and we admire them.

Sometimes we feel different from the rest of our family. In my seminars I ask, "Who has more than one child?"

A number of people raise their hands. Then I ask, "Are they the same?"

Nearly everyone shakes their head no. We are born with different temperaments.

What if you are a pit bull born into a family of collies? What is going to be your role in the family? You may hear things like, "You are too aggressive. Why do you have to be such a bully? You are so insensitive." You take the role of the black sheep.

What if you are a collie born into a family of pit bulls? Now you are going to hear things like, "You are too sensitive. Can't you ever stand up for yourself? You are such a wimp."

So, you see, temperaments are very important. Research shows that temperament is a significant factor in hostility. Now let's apply temperaments to "orientation"—or how a person is based mentally. Most of us have a primary orientation in reflection, cognition, or emotion (physical). It is a simple way of explaining the mental functions applied to the temperament.

Orientation	Productive Side	Dark Side	Positive Examples
Reflective	Sees big picture	Power thirsty	Captain Kate Janeway
	Best for all	Best for me	
Cognitive	Understanding	Invalidative	Number 7 of 9 Borg
	Accommodating	Pompous	
Emotional/ Physical	Affectionate	Physically abusive	Worf the Klingon
	Attentive	Emotionally abusive	

I used characters from Star Trek and related series rather than real people for examples. These characters can be seen in action films if you wish to study their temperaments further.

The orientation is the primary mental processor. Everyone has a mammal (emotional/physical) processor, a logic (cognitive) processor, and a prefrontal lobe (reflective processor). It is just that they may get their strongest motivations from the mental processor. For them, that's the primary one.

A person who is physically oriented may have the ability to think and reflect on the bigger picture but is more comfortable on the emotional/physical level. This person takes cues from touch and raw emotions. I saw an interaction between a cognitive stoic male and an emotionally oriented female. I knew he liked her, and she asked him over for coffee. He stoically said yes in his monotone voice, and she immediately jumped up and said, "If you don't really want to go, then tell me no."

It surprised him, and he showed a little emotion then and said, "No, I really do want to go!" She saw the puppy dog in his eyes and then smiled and said OK. She read the non-verbal messages, while he was oriented toward cognitive word-oriented communication. She mistook his stoicism for a lack of interest when he was actually very interested. They ended up learning a lot from each other.

One of the possible disorders of the physically oriented temperament may be ADHD. People diagnosed with ADHD may not think in full sentences and they may not be very cognitive. Their Chihuahua temperament barks a lot and gets distracted by every movement and every noise. It is estimated that more than 30 percent of kids with ADHD "outgrow" it in adolescence. This may not be exactly true. It may be that the prefrontal lobe starts working around that time and they become situationally aware. They are then able to oversee the mammal and put a leash on that overactive Chihuahua temperament.

A person who is cognitively oriented is logically oriented. Her most powerful cues come from logic (e.g., science and technology). She may be able to see the bigger picture, but she doesn't enjoy being in charge. She may be able to understand emotions, but she tries to keep hers private. She may not enjoy a lot of physical contact unless it is expected or previously planned. Mania makes a person excessively cognitive. When a woman is manic, she is having racing thoughts. Her prefrontal lobe is not operating at maximum efficiency (if at all), and she is not in touch with her feelings. To come out of the mania, she needs to be in touch with her feelings and see the bigger picture of what is happening.

A reflective woman may have had access to her prefrontal lobe at an early age. Psychiatrist and author Alice Miller calls these folks gifted when they are children because they seem to have an objective awareness at a young age. These women are usually the ones who put their finger in the hole in the dam. They are the peacekeepers. They try to make up for the family dysfunctions. If this person goes bad, though, she can think of ingenious ways to twist the bigger picture and make others look bad. She can set up others to fall, and the person who falls may have no idea what happened. Whether she is on the positive side or the dark side, she is *situationally aware*. On the dark side, this is the woman who gossips about you behind your back and swears everyone to secrecy. She may make you look like "the poor thing," and she will pretend to have sympathy for you to others. But when the promotion comes up, she gets it even though you knew you were more qualified. She is the one who may do the same thing in your personal life. She may distort things to your friends secretly and be so nice to your face, but eventually they are all meeting at her house and you don't get invited. She may treat you like a Madonna and put you up on a pedestal in front of your man, all the while setting you up to take him away from you. On the good side, with the right ethics and upbringing, she can be an excellent role model and leader with foresight and good intent.

Damaged Goods

Damage is defined as an injury to a person. Goods are favorable characteristics or qualities. So we are talking about an injury to a good part of a person. One thing that damages the good parts of a human being is abuse. It could be sexual abuse, physical abuse, emotional abuse, verbal abuse, or neglect. Here are two examples of situations where women were abused and that damage led them to act in ways that might classify them as "nasty women." These examples are all part of understanding others, which will lead us to the "what to do" process.

There were three sisters who went to a therapist. All three had been molested by the same person. The oldest sister remembered everything. The middle sister remembered going into his room and coming out, but she didn't remember what happened. The youngest didn't remember anything.

During one session, the middle sister came to the session upset. She had gotten angry at her husband the night before and treated him viciously. She was in her late twenties, which is the age that sexual abuse in childhood may become symptomatic. She couldn't understand why she had been so awful with him. She knew him to be a caring and loving man. The therapist asked her what happened. She told the therapist that her husband had just come over to sit down with her on the couch. They were watching television and he started holding her hand. She found herself going into a tirade, telling him that he was a pervert and that he better not think that he was going to have sex with her. The therapist asked if that was his signal that he wanted sex. She told the therapist, "No. He just wanted to hold my hand."

Then the oldest one spoke up and said, "I know why you reacted that way." She continued, "When we went into the room, he [the molester] would turn on the TV and after we started watching it, he would start by holding our hand and then go on to do his thing."

The middle sister didn't remember it, but her mammal did.

The reason these things start coming up in the late twenties or early thirties is because a woman is mature enough to deal with them then. The mammal wants to purge the emotional content of the trauma. It is burdensome to carry around the emotional charge and keep it in the unconscious. She becomes symptomatic of the trauma and may think she is going crazy, but with the right help, she is actually going sane.

In another case, a woman was date raped by her fiancé. She didn't tell anyone because her parents liked him. She broke off the engagement two weeks before the wedding, which upset people in both families. She was devastated by the rape and was dealing with that at the same time she was dealing with everyone's ridicule for calling off the wedding at such a late time. She could barely respond to them and just kept saying, "I just don't want to."

Her fiancé had the typical rape mentality and believed she teased him and then was sorry afterward but that she really asked for it. Her family allowed him to vent his verbal abuse on her, thinking that she deserved it.

She immediately took up with a male friend she had known for years, and on the day that would have been her wedding day, she and the male friend ran off to the Caribbean. Prior to her leaving for the Caribbean, her father slapped her in the face and disowned her. She was in such a state of shock from everything that she showed no emotion. Her friend knew she wasn't herself and was very gentle with her and endearing. She broke down emotionally on the vacation, and he was there for her; they formed a strong bond. When she returned from vacation, her belongings were outside on the porch.

She was normally a very responsible person who did all the right things. It was so out of character for her to jilt a fiancé and run off with another man. Why did her family react the way they did? Several factors led to their responses: narcissism (taking it personally), misunderstanding, and not taking the time to go into the prefrontal lobe long enough to see the big picture and realize that she wasn't following her normal characteristic responses.

Brain Chemicals

A small understanding of brain chemistry can also contribute to our understanding of what makes a woman nasty.

There may be actual physiological (chemical) causes of conditions that lead to nastiness rather than just nastiness for no reason. A certain "craziness" (internal rage) goes along with a chemical imbalance, and if you can maintain your awareness and not take it personally, you can actually see (feel) it. For example, research shows that a lack of serotonin in the brain can cause a person to be depressed or hostile. In seasonal affective disorder, the lack of serotonin can make a person more agitated during the wintertime than during summer. If you are looking for the bigger picture, you can be aware that this person has problems in the winter. What causes this lack of serotonin?

Research has found that when the iris of the eye is subjected to sunlight, it signals the brain to start manufacturing serotonin. After the sun goes down, the brain switches to producing melatonin, the hormone found in a hibernating bear's body. During the winter, due to the shorter days, some people do not get enough serotonin. These people have a bad time during the winter months. The pattern in their lives may be that they have the most marital discord during the winter. They argue more and are hostile. Wintertime is when they lose their jobs. So what's the cure? It may sound weird, but if they expose themselves to special lights that put out the same spectrum of light as the sun does, they do just fine. It is a physiological depression rather than a psychological depression.

Others have a physiological depression that runs in the family. They may need a serotonin vitamin like Prozac, Paxil, or Zoloft. I call them "serotonin vitamins" because they are not like the old drugs. They are not blockers or anesthetizers.

A lack of serotonin is usually the cause of a physiological depression. But there is another chemical imbalance that is still not very well understood in our society. This chemical imbalance can make people ornery and nasty, or depressed. In this book, I am talking about the nasty stuff, so I will concentrate on that part.

There are many people who have the bipolar disorder. It used to be called manic-depression. It is extremely important that you know about this chemical imbalance if you really want to deal with nasty women, because there are plenty of women (and men) who have this problem. Many of them are very functional and could be called "soft bipolar." You have met this bipolar woman. You may as well be able to deal with her. You don't have to be a shrink to understand her.

Bipolar disorder is a chemical and hereditary problem. A person could be of sound psychological makeup, and this disorder would make him or her appear to be crazy (intense, rageful, euphoric). Most people do not understand this disorder. Even therapists, psychiatrists, psychologists, social workers, and people who have the disorder do not understand it completely. They understand it enough to do their job, but there is a lot more they could know. Many people who are bipolar get a bad rap. Remember twenty years ago when we thought that alcoholics were just weak willed? We are in the same situation with bipolar disorder—about

twenty years behind what we should be for the treatment
and thirty years behind in the way we respond to the people who have it.

I believe there is a bipolar temperament, and when this
temperament gets out of whack, we call it the bipolar disorder. People with the disorder may be hardworking. They
like to keep busy. They can be brilliant. They are usually
very intelligent. They can attend to details. They can be
very creative. They may think six times faster than others
and get impatient with people who don't think or talk as
fast as they do. They can think "out of the box." They can
be witty and charming and have a great sense of humor.
They tend to be truthful, and they can be a lot of fun.

On the other side, they can be very angry. It is a manic-
anger and it is accompanied by an agitation. When they are
manicly angry, they are still thinking six times faster than
you are, and they can say things that will rip your heart out.
During this mania, their conscience is at the back door of
their mind. They talk fast and feel pressured to keep talking. They will tell you things you don't want to know. They
will tell you things that might get them in trouble. They
may become hypersexual. What is hypersexual? If you
remember when you were an adolescent and you had trouble resisting sexual urges . . . multiply that by ten and see
if you can resist. They do things when they are manic that
destroy their lives. They run up their credit cards, or use
drugs, or gamble away their life savings, or contract a sexual disease. They may cheat on their spouse. After they stop

being manic, their conscience comes back and they are remorseful, if not suicidal. They don't sleep much when manic, and they have mood swings. Their thoughts race. They are not in touch with their feelings, and their prefrontal lobe capability is reduced or not operational. They don't see the consequences of what they are doing, and they don't see the bigger picture. They may seem brilliant in the details of things, but they lack judgment (judgment is a prefrontal lobe capability). They may not be able to stop being angry. If you let them punch a punching bag to get their anger out of their system, they will punch that bag from now until next Tuesday and never get it out of their system. It is a physical rage that sweeps them up.

What can be done for them? Well, before diabetics had insulin, the public was afraid of them. A diabetic who was having a low-blood-sugar attack could be as mean as anything. A diabetic could have "fits" (convulsions).

The "insulin" for a bipolar is a mood stabilizer. There are plenty of good mood stabilizers, and they work well for most bipolars. Some do not respond completely to the medications we have at this time, just as some diabetics have a difficult time keeping their sugar balanced with insulin because their system is so erratic.

The secret to controlling diabetes is a good diet, whereas the secret to controlling the bipolar disorder is getting good sleep. Bipolars get nasty because they don't get enough sleep. The bipolar disorder is not a psychotic illness so much as it causes the person to become sleep deprived. Any normal person who stopped sleeping would eventually become psychotic to some degree. Any person who didn't get enough sleep would probably get irritable and nasty. Add mood swings and racing thoughts, and you have a nasty combination. With bipolar women, you sometimes have the additional stress of a hormonal effect. Think about it. Let's say on a particular day a woman was suffering from all of the following:

1. A lack of sleep
2. A chemical imbalance causing racing thoughts, causing mood swings, and causing her brain to be directly connected to her tongue
3. A nonoperational prefrontal lobe so her judgment is poor and she has no filtering system (research, through PET scans, shows little activity in the prefrontal lobe when a person is manic)
4. Symptoms of PMS, including retaining water

Let's see anyone with all that get through the day without cutting somebody up! Most women would understand. Another woman might see that this was a bad day for the woman experiencing the symptoms. Most men wouldn't understand. A man might think of her as a bitch and make judgments about her. Some women might think she is extreme and should be able to control herself more than she does (not realizing the bipolar factors). Even she herself might notice the intensity and think that she should be able to handle it. But she can't. Did I say "can't"? Oh good, because I didn't mean to say "won't." I meant to say "can't."

The word *can't* changes things, you see. It means that you can't take personally all those nasty things she said to you while her brain was connected to her tongue, no matter how biting, heartrending, and unconscionable they were (but you probably will anyway). It means that she should be allowed to forgive herself for having outbursts beyond her control (but if she realizes this, she has to also recognize the need for a mood stabilizer). I believe that people with the soft bipolar disorder can be trusted to take their mood stabilizers as needed. The mood stabilizers are not addictive, and some are actually extracts rather than synthetic drugs. Someone who is severely manic (as compared to moderately manic and mildly manic) has poor judgment and must rely on others for help in reminding her or him to take the medication. Of course, that person will probably resist the help because of the trilogy she experiences—egocentrism, arrogance, entitlement—when she is manic. If your boss, wife, lover, mother, or someone close to you has these elements, it might help to read *Bipolar Disorder* by Francis Mark Mondimore, or at least get my handbook *Bipolar* on the jaycarter.net website.

If you have a close relationship with this person, you may find that she has many redeeming qualities. She can be affectionate and endearing. She can be efficient and effective. She may get five days of work done in one day. Then other times, it takes her five days to get one day's work done. She can be a lot of fun. She is adventurous and may get you to do things you wouldn't ordinarily do (but are glad you did). It may be important that this person go on medication for the mood swings, manic-anger, racing thoughts, and lack of sleep. This medication would be a mood stabilizer, most likely. Maybe you would be able to help her be compliant with the medication because your prefrontal lobe may be operational most of the time, even though sometimes hers is not.

If she is a boss or coworker of yours, you can be reassured that you should not take personally things she says when she is manic-angry. If you look for it, you should be able to tell if she is genuinely angry at you or not. There will be a "craziness" to it if she is manic; she will have a physical agitation. Just try to stay away from her until the mood passes, which it will because it is a mood swing and may not have anything to do with you. To think otherwise might be narcissistic. She is not like the blowfish (Ms. Bullee), although her behavior may look the same sometimes. The origin of her behavior is purely chemical. The origin of the blowfish's behavior is usually early family dysfunction. She may also resemble the flounder (Ms. Unpredictable) in behavior sometimes. It's just temporary.

After she dumps on you, she may be apologetic the next day. She does have a conscience and a prefrontal lobe. They just dim with the manic energy.

There was a mildly bipolar woman I knew who ran a business. She had many employees working for her. She told everyone not to come into her office in the mornings, because she was usually in a bad mood. For some reason, people would go into her office in the morning anyway, like cattle to a slaughter. She would scream and yell at them for asking for a day off. They would walk out, all beaten down with chins on the floor. By the afternoon, she usually cheered up, and many times she would seek out the people she had yelled at and tell them they could have the day off. In the afternoon, her prefrontal lobe was operating well, and she could "think out of the box" and come up with a way to let these people take off. She was happy-manic most of the year (except for the mornings) but would always get full-blown manic during January and February. That was the only time she would take medication. The psychiatrist sat down with her and her husband, and they came up with a plan that if the psychiatrist told her to, she would take her medication for at least two months. Everyone loved January and February. She was laid-back and easygoing when she was on her medication. She would sleep twelve hours a day. Sometimes she wouldn't even go to work. She wasn't in anyone's face. Her employees and husband could take a break from her high-intensity, fast-paced self. But she hated it. She complained that it slowed her down. It *did* slow her down but only to normal where the rest of us mortals are down here on earth. She said it interfered with her creativity. Maybe, but it stopped her from ruining her life over that two-month period. After two months on the medication, she had the morale back at the business and her husband was rested up. She was rested up and ready for the next hypomanic ten months.

Most people know someone with some or all of these traits. Now you know where it comes from—a chemical disorder.

What can you do about it? Any of the following in any order:

- Be sympathetic even when she is angry and stabbing you with tongue daggers. (You can do this only if you don't take it personally.)
- Show her you like her. She responds to affinity.
- Avoid her when she is angry-manic. (It will pass.)
- Don't let her go on and on when she is angry-manic. She can't stop. Crack a joke or change the subject.
- Remind her of the bigger picture (get her forward in her prefrontal lobe).
- Make her laugh. She may respond to a sense of humor and the humor lightens things up, getting things back into perspective (perspective comes from the prefrontal lobe).

Find the Stick

There is an old story about a master and a student. The student goes to the master's house and the master invites her in. She sits down at a table with a cup of tea on it. The master pulls out a big stick from under the table and says, "Here is your lesson for the day. If you drink that cup of tea, I will hit you with this stick, and if you don't drink that cup of tea, I will hit you with this stick."

This problem cannot be solved with the logic processor. The logic says things like, "Well, I would drink the tea because I may as well enjoy it if I am going to get hit anyway." Others say, "I would dump the tea [they would then get hit]." Or, "I would throw it in the master's face. If the SOB is going to hit me, I may as well get him too."

It is not a *logical* problem. It is a situational problem. It's the bigger picture that has to be solved. It is not about the tea. Get it?

OK, some say they would leave. That shows they may be using their prefrontal lobe and they are changing the situation. But it could be they are just getting the heck out of there because they have figured out that they are going to get hit with the stick anyway. One mammal-logic-oriented person said that she would tell the master, "If that stick starts coming down on me, I am going to kick you in a place that will make you sing soprano."

These answers are all very interesting, but the best answer is . . . take the stick away. By taking the stick away, you can change the relationship with the master but still remain connected.

The master is setting up a double-bind situation—a predicament in which it seems a person can't win no matter what he or she does. We feel the worst when we get into a double-bind situation. There is always a negative feeling that goes with it. Trust that feeling. It is trying to tell you there is something wrong. Now pay attention to this section. This little section here is going to save you such grief in your life that it would be worth it to study this section for hours or days. I am asking you for only a couple of minutes, but do not discount it just because I have taken the trouble to boil it down for you. This one little section is going to make it worth whatever you paid for this book and a little of your time. What I am trying to say is, *this is important*!

Step 1. Feel the feeling. The feeling of anger you get when you are in a situation that seems to have ill effects no matter what you do is important. It's trying to tell you something. It's trying to tell you what you already know. It's trying to tell you that you *are* in a double-bind situation.

Step 2. Once you realize you are in a double-bind situation, forget about trying to figure it out for a moment. Take a deep breath, stop your mind from racing, and just look at it. (Meditate on it, see it, or however you want to say it.) Allow yourself to feel it. What does it feel like? Write down on paper what you think your options are. Then look at all those options. Don't think on them, just look. See anything? If not, we need to make you bigger than that situation.

Pretend for a moment that you are a super-being flying through space and you happen to come upon this planet with billions of people on it. You want to check out just one of these people, and you happen to observe the very person reading this book right now. You look over this person's current moment, taking into consideration the life span, past, and anticipated future of this person. What do you see? What advice would you give to this person? If the person is in a double-bind situation, *what is the stick*?

There was a well-off woman I knew who had a sister. Her sister was a single mother who lived on the other side of town with three children from three different men. The sister would remind her, "Mom didn't love me as much as you, and that is why I didn't do as well. You have all this money. It won't kill you to help me." This put the woman in a quandary. She didn't want to enable her sister (but she did enable her). She didn't want to abandon her, either. It was true about their mom. One time the sister said, "I need to get away on a vacation. You get away all the time. You need to send me to Hawaii." The woman refused. Her sister said, "If you can't do that for me with all the money you have, don't bother coming here anymore. So you choose." Well, she loved her sister's kids, and she was a good influence on them. She didn't want to give that up. She had been the surrogate mother for her sister since their mother rejected her. So what should she do? What was the stick? The dysfunctional relationship? OK, but what specifically? Using the children? OK, but what specifically? Playing mom to her? OK, but what specifically? The stick is always something we can work with. It is not the dysfunction. *The stick is the choice.*

Simple, huh? If you didn't get it, you weren't in your prefrontal lobe. The woman said to her sister, "I am not going to choose. You choose. Do you want me in your life or not?" The responsibility for the choice fell back on the sister, who wasn't very responsible and so didn't choose.

We are not done yet. It's time to demonstrate the situation.

Demonstrate the Situation

State the facts. Just say it the way it is. Do a Joe Friday thing. It's the truth and the whole truth. Rules: while demonstrating the situation to someone, do not:

- Judge
- Criticize
- Give your opinion
- Invalidate the other
- Make value judgments
- Use adjectives
- Use exclamation marks (verbally)
- Attack character
- Be defensive
- Label
- Blame

- Be hostile
- Reject
- Threaten
- Abandon
- Intimidate
- Dominate
- Move to immediately solve the problem
- Get caught up thinking badly of the other or of the other's ulterior motives

Do:

- Use "I" statements vs. "you" statements (e.g., "I feel angry" vs. "you tick me off")
- Seek progress, not solution, not perfection
- Be direct but tactful
- Notice the other person's mood/feelings, eyes, situation
- Demand respect from the person
- Show respect
- Listen

All this takes practice. You will probably not get it right the first time. This is a process, not an end product. You will get better and better at doing this. If you are ready for all this, then it's time to demonstrate the situation. So the woman in our previous example would say to her sister, "Let me understand this. You want me to pay for your trip to Hawaii. If I don't, then I can't see you anymore. That means I won't be able to see the sister I grew up with, my nephew, or my nieces. That would hurt me because I love them. I think they love me too, and I think you love me. You feel like I should do this because I have plenty of money. You feel that Mom favored me and that's another reason I should do this. Do I have that correctly?"

What she has done is to take her sister into the prefrontal lobe. If this is successful, the sister will see the bigger picture and it may end here. If not, she may have to go further. If she goes further, she must stick to her feelings: "I feel sad and scared, and there is something about this I don't feel right about."

If the sister stands her ground, the woman must tell her she can't talk to her right now. She is too upset. They will have to talk later. That gives the sister a chance to mull it over and the woman a chance to reflect on the situation. Take note. There wasn't a situation, and then there *was*. The sister has a situation and she is putting it onto this woman. It's not about the trip to Hawaii and it's not about any of the following:

- The sister's manipulation
- Not seeing the sister's kids
- Mom not favoring the sister
- All the woman has done for the sister
- The woman's guilt
- The sister's entitlement

- The sister's pain
- The woman's pain
- The woman's responsibility
- The sister's irresponsibility

It's about none of that! At the moment, it's about the *choice* to enable the sister or not.

If you look at this predicament circumstantially, it looks like it's about these things. If the woman makes a decision based on circumstances, the situation will keep coming up. If she makes a situational decision, she is not playing into the circumstances.

I need to take a little time here to explain the difference between circumstantial decisions and situational decisions. I could have picked two other words, but I chose *circumstance* and *situation* to explain a very important perspective. I am not sure that the English language has the exact words that could explain this perspective, so I am bastardizing these two words to get the point across.

I define a circumstance as an event. It is like circumstantial evidence. It doesn't contain the bigger picture. It's just a snapshot. It is *content*. I define a situation as the big picture. The whole nine yards including future repercussions. It is the *context*.

If you go to a friend's house and he or she asks you if you want a beer, your decision is probably going to be a circumstantial one. "Do I want a beer?" If, however, you are an alcoholic who is on the wagon, it is not a circumstantial decision; it is a situational decision. "Do I want to ruin my life?" Having a beer is not a double-bind situation for most people. For an alcoholic, it is. The alcoholic's past has many circumstantial decisions that add up to a pattern of his or her life becoming unmanageable.

The woman who feels like she is held hostage from her sister's children by being manipulated by her sister is facing a situational decision. She could just say, "OK. Here's the money. Go to Hawaii." This would approach it circumstantially, but what would happen to the bigger picture? Resentment, manipulation, and more hostage-holding would be a part of the ongoing relationship.

Let's take a very extreme example. Let's say a sadistic criminal breaks into your house and tells you to decide which of your family members to shoot first. If you make the circumstantial decision, you are agreeing to participate in the situation created by the sadistic killer. He is in control. You see, the situation is already there anyway. A sadistic killer has broken into your house. If you choose, you are involved in his context. He is going to do whatever he is going to do *anyway*. By not choosing, you are not in his control . . . and he wants you in his control so he can force you to take responsibility. I have met a couple of sadistic killers. If they can control you, they lose respect for you. Your only chance to live is to have him respect you. Beg for mercy and you are dead. He may kill you anyway, but the responsibility will be on him. Sadistic killers (and other people) don't like to take responsibility for what they do. But that is a separate issue. It doesn't matter what the psychology of a sadistic killer is. You need to make a situational response, not a circumstantial response.

Here is another example that demonstrates how we make situational decisions based on circumstance. People fall in love. What do they do when they fall in love, sometimes? They get married. It's a situational response to a circumstantial feeling. People shouldn't get married because they are in love. They get married because they want that lifestyle. I don't mean to sound cold. I am not cold, but I have seen so many failed marriages. People who are not meant for each other and people who are not meant for a married lifestyle get married. Maybe it's Mother Nature's way of ensuring the next crop of babies. I don't know. What does it mean when you love someone? It means that you love that person. That's all. I am not belittling love. Love is probably the most meaningful experience we can have on this earth. Love has meaning in and of itself, and love should not translate into marriage all the time. In the United States, we have very little prefrontal lobe capability when it comes to marriage. Marriage should be chosen because we want *that* situation for our lives. I realize that it may be hard to coordinate falling in love at the same time we want to get married, but come on. It's a process, isn't it? If the decision to marry would include an objective consultation with people who knew one or the other or both, then there would be some prefrontal lobes looking at the marriage potential. That might work well. In our culture, sometimes we have the mammals mating, which is then followed by nuptials. I have heard people who are from responsibly arranged marriages say, "We got married and *then* we fell in love." We put ourselves in a double-bind situation when we look at it as "Whoops, I fell in love. I guess we better get married." We end up making a situational decision (without realizing it) without really *seeing* the situation and without understanding that it is a decision that affects the rest of our lives. We approach it as a circumstantial decision, which it is *not*.

So back to the sister. She is obviously holding the woman hostage, justifying it, and blaming her for it. So what?! The circumstances are not as important as the situation. If you are going to start dealing with nasty women, you may need to make situational decisions, not circumstantial ones.

For a man who works for a woman who hates men, the situation matters, not whatever circumstances happen to pop up. When she passes him over for promotion, she may have some very good reasons. So what? Things will never be right unless he changes his situation and works for someone who is not a misandrist. Until he makes that situational decision, he will never know how good he is. There are usually other jobs and other bosses, unless there are other redeeming facets in his situation with her.

A woman who works for a female boss who favors men is in a *situation*, not a *circumstance*. She has to decide if she likes it there enough to stay. There may be other redeeming benefits.

It may be difficult to discern the difference between a situational decision and a circumstantial decision, yet sometimes the situational decision is the one that is going to get you closer to the situation you prefer in life. In order to make a situational decision, you must see the reality of the situation and not get caught up in the circumstances. For example, the battered woman who situationally is married to a batterer, but who circumstantially needs an income for herself and her children, has nowhere else to live. A situational decision is long term. A circumstantial decision is for the time being. Please don't get caught up in the words I use, but try to see the bigger picture I am trying to convey. A situation is marked by a pattern, whereas a circumstance is a one-shot deal. If I am married to someone who opposes everything I do and never shows affection, those are two patterns defining my situation. The circumstances may be, "We can't afford for you to go to night school" (oppositional) or, "Don't touch me, I just did my nails" (no affection). These circumstances may change to, "I am not in the mood to have your friend over," (oppositional) or, "Don't hold my hand; you are distracting me" or, "Don't! I am watching this movie" (no affection). The *situational* pattern will remain the same.

If you get good at it, you can spot a pattern almost the first time it happens: "I know we just met and this is embarrassing, but could I borrow ten bucks?"

Did I give you enough examples yet? Well, we are not done. I want to give you something to take with you for the remainder of your days. It is the bottom line for most situations, but it isn't a line. It's a process. Continue please.

The Universal Resolution

Would you rather I gave you a whole bunch of concrete lists for you to memorize so that you could address your circumstances concretely? Or would you rather have me give you one thing—one magical process that works all the time? If you have this magical process, you will be able to make up your own lists, personalized and customized to fit you.

The magic is not a "poof" magic. It is a process, one that is guaranteed to unfold you and take you to the next level. It is a simple process but maybe not easy all the time. This process gets you into your prefrontal lobe more often and makes you more and more aware. If you use this process, you will get better and better every day. So it's not "instant pudding," but it will work. Guaranteed. And you will get more out of it than pudding. You will get more out of it than just the ability to solve a particular momentary circumstance.

Just follow me for a while. It may seem disjointed but it will come together in the end. I am going to talk about charisma. You have seen charisma in others (not the con artist type of charisma but true charisma). It seems a person with charisma can always deal with circumstances. This person comes from a situational perspective. This person always sees the bigger picture. He or she can be confronted with the most unusual circumstance and seem to handle it. Take any of the fish in the sea—women with chemical problems, abused women—and this charismatic person can deal with them. It's not because of *what* he or she knows. It's because of *who* he or she is. I believe all of us have our own brand of charisma. We have it when we are children, and then we get invalidated and traumatized and lose it. Except . . . we never really lose it. It just gets covered over by circumstances. It's not that some people are born with "it" and others aren't. So what qualities does a charismatic person have? I do seminars across the United States for hundreds of people, and no matter where I am, the answers are the same. A person with charisma has these characteristics:

- Is magnetic
- Hears you
- Is interested (rather than trying to be interesting)
- Makes you feel liked
- Shows respect
- Is motivated
- Is passionate about what he or she does
- Is optimistic
- Has a sense of humor
- Is confident
- Is honest but tactful

- Is direct but tactful
- Is genuine
- Has no ulterior motives
- Is personable

Dealing with nasty women is more effective with "being-ness" rather than "doingness." As a manager at IBM Corp., I remember two people who worked for me. One was very charismatic. The other was the best technician. The best technician would show up at a customer location, fix the problem, and leave. He fixed more equipment than anyone, but I had more complaints about him than anyone. He had poor people skills. The one with charisma admitted that he wasn't that good at fixing equipment, but the customers loved him and I never had a complaint. He would say hello to the customer, listen with empathy, and try very hard to satisfy him or her. He was a communicator. When a management position became available, guess who got it? The communicator. It was based more on who he was (being-ness) rather than what he did (doingness). He was competent in fixing equipment, not exceptional. But he was exceptional in dealing with people.

That's why a person with charisma can handle a nasty woman and others so well.

Now, I would never ask you to be someone that you aren't. That wouldn't be good. But I would ask you to be who you are and be *more* of who you are. Have you ever met a child who didn't have her or his own little brand of charisma? All the children I have ever met have had charisma. So you know we all have it . . . ever so buried as it may be.

How do we get our charisma back to help us deal with nasty women and other situations? OK. You want the shortcut? Yes, of course you do. If you want the shortcut, then you have to trust me a little, otherwise I have to write another hundred pages to explain why this works. So here it is:

Let's suppose you were mulling around in your prefrontal lobe one day and decided that among the strategies of your life were going to be to show affinity, acknowledge feelings, and genuinely admire people *no matter what.*

How would others take that? Well, what if someone showed you affinity (shook your hand, touched you appropriately, smiled at you, etc.)? What if someone acknowledged your feelings and you could see that this person was genuinely looking for your feelings and interested in your feelings? What if this person found something to admire about you (something real)? How would that make you feel? Most people would say it would make them feel good. Would you be inclined to hurt a person like this? Probably not.

OK, good for the receiver, but what about the giver? If you did this, what kind of a person would you turn out to be?

1. You would be someone who tried to show caring and affection to others.

2. You would be someone who was interested in other people. (You would have to be to find their feelings.)
3. You would be someone who would see the good in people. (You would have to be in order to find something to admire.)

If you were doing 1, 2, and 3, you would be too busy to do other things people might do instead, like judge, criticize, notice faults, avoid, and so on. The beauty of this is that it doesn't take up any more of your time. You are already doing something. You just do this instead. If we let ourselves do what we have always done, then we just repeat it over and over. Our old tapes (old methods) don't erase, but we can record over them. A strategy in the prefrontal lobe overrides almost everything (although not perfectly at first). With practice, we get better and better. So here are our strategies:

- Maintain a situational awareness.
- Don't take things personally.
- Show affinity.
- Acknowledge feelings.
- Find something to admire.

These are strategies, *not rules*. If you think of them as rules, then you're not originating your thought in the prefrontal lobe, you are in the logic processor. You have to make these things part of your *being*. A strategy is something in the back of your mind all the time. What is in back (or should I say in forward) of your mind? The prefrontal lobe.

Ever go on a diet? Maybe you were good for a couple of days and then cheated. Then you said to yourself, "I blew it. I may as well pig out now." That's because you were approaching the diet from the logic processor instead of from the prefrontal lobe (circumstantially instead of situationally). In the logic processor, everything is black and white. It's all or nothing. In the prefrontal lobe processor, it's an intent. Your strategy takes in the situation. So you might say, "Darn, I had that donut. I shouldn't have done that." But you lift yourself up, dust yourself off, and stay on the diet. If you have a donut every day, you notice that and then use the logic processor to figure out how not to have that donut. "Gee, I stop at the donut store for my coffee every day. Maybe I should buy my coffee somewhere else." Otherwise you are taking the mammal in the donut shop every day, and the mammal smells the donuts, sees the donuts, and is going to have a donut. The logic is no help because the mammal overrides the logic (obvious in this case). So all the logic will do is watch the mammal break the diet rules and then criticize the mammal for it, or justify having the donut. The black and white of the logic doesn't understand the mammal.

Another example:

Let's suppose you enact the strategies I've given you. There you are at work talking to some coworkers and Ms.

Bullee comes up and snaps at you, "Did you get my E-mail about the urgency of Project ABC?" That comment has a lot of innuendos. Some of them are "There you are standing around talking when you have urgent work to do. You are irresponsible, undedicated, and philandering your time. Obviously I have a right to be upset with you." These kinds of innuendos tend to make people introverted. You might say to yourself, "Oh! Am I being irresponsible (self-doubt)? I am embarrassed about what my coworkers are going to think. It looks like I am philandering my time. Ms. Bullee just made me look bad, after I worked so hard for her this week." If you take it personally, you may put your head down and with all your introversion and self-doubt say, "I'm sorry. I'll work on it right now." Or if you take it personally, you may get defensive and say, "But . . . but . . . I have been working on it all week and it's almost done" (trying to explain to her and your coworkers that you are not irresponsible and undedicated). If you are of a different temperament, you might bark back at her.

Otherwise, if you stick to our strategies, you would do the following:

1. Maintain a situational awareness (look at her, see how others are affected, etc.).
2. Not take it personally (not become introverted, not let your self-doubt cave you in).
3. Show affinity (touch her appropriately, smile).

4. Acknowledge her feelings ("You really feel under the gun about that project, huh?").

5. Admire her ("I don't mind working for someone like you. What do you need?").

Keep practicing and watch what happens in a month, a year. If life gets much better, write me a note. My address is in this book.

To tide you over until you get better at the process, there are three major concrete things that seem to work in most situations.

1. **The repeater technique.** If you can't think of anything clever to say in 6.5 seconds, you say, "What did you say?" Whatever they said to you, they won't say it the same way a second time. It stops them and makes them think. They know they are "caught." You are confronting them, and most people don't like to be confronted.

2. **Get them alone.** People who embarrass you in front of others usually get scared when confronted alone. Chances are they won't embarrass you in front of a group again.

3. **Make them situationally aware.** Many times, people have had their buttons pushed and are not in present time. You just make them aware of their surroundings. "Your eyes are getting all red. You are

raising your voice at me. I am feeling intimidated. Is this what you want?"

The Big Picture

Here is where we take the entirety of the book and put it into the big picture. The most important part of the book was the discussion about committed-mate relationships. This is where there are missed understandings:

- A man hands over a part of his self-esteem to his wife/partner for safekeeping. Once he does this, it becomes very important to him what she thinks of him.
- A woman marries a man for his potential and works hard to help him be the man that she knows he can be.
- A woman tries to be intimate with a man by sharing her feelings.
- A man tries to bare his soul by showing her his hopes and dreams.
- The man thinks the woman is putting pins in his jujube doll (self-esteem) when she is actually trying to get him to live up to his potential.
- A woman tries to get a man to share his feelings so that they become more intimate when that is not necessarily intimate to a man. A man tries to get a

woman to show her intent or purpose, when she is trying to get her feelings acknowledged.

The fix for this is to turn the missed understanding into an understanding.

The second most important part of the book is to uncover our charisma. We all had our own brand of charisma as children, but then it was buried under an onslaught of trauma, invalidation, criticism, self-doubt, and other evil mechanisms. We were too innocent to stop it, then. But now we are wiser and we have perspective. We can uncover our charisma through the process of:

- Affinity
- Acknowledgment
- Admiration

This process (if we work at it) uncovers our charisma, and as it does we feel more and more like our true self, more genuine, more real, more loving, less introverted, less doubtful, more passionate, more energetic. We don't have time to introvert, cave in, or be filled with self-doubt because we are looking "out there" and directing our energy "out there," showing affinity to others, acknowledging others, and admiring others.

When we start the process, it may not feel real and we may have to "fake it until we make it." We might start off with ulterior motives for developing charisma (raises, promotions, getting people to like us, and so forth). But to carry out the strategies (affinity, acknowledgment, admiration), we have to genuinely try to connect with people, genuinely be interested in people to see what they are feeling, and genuinely see the good in people so we can admire them. We get better and better every day and better and better in every way.

Statistics show that it doesn't matter whether a person is forced to go to a rehab or whether they volunteer. The cure rate is the same. By the same token, it doesn't matter if your motives for getting back your charisma are good or not. The result is the same in the end. With charisma, a person can handle a nasty woman in the most optimum way possible (if she can be handled). If she is unmanageable, that will soon become apparent if you have directed your energy "out there" where she is, instead of "in there" where all your self-doubt, trauma, and introversion lie. Did I say "lie"? What a great pun! And meant both ways.

The rest of the information is just information, and you can refer to this book anytime for that. Take these processes, work them, and see if your life improves a little each day, a lot in a year, and immensely in a couple years. Let's concentrate on who you are rather than what you do. Let's concentrate on beingness rather than doingness. The doingness will take care of itself with the beingness of being who you really are. And don't forget: you *are* your relationships.

I hope this book starts these processes, which means you are going to take them with you. Send me a note to let me how you are doing or even to scold me if you need to.

Bibliography

Alpert, R. *Be Here Now*. San Cristobal, N.Mex.: Lama Foundation, 1971.

American Psychological Association. *Warning Signs*. Washington, D.C.: American Psychological Association, 2000.

Augsburger, David. *When Caring Is Not Enough*. Ventura, Calif.: Regal Books, 1983.

Augustine Fellowship. *Sex and Love Addicts Anonymous*. Boston: Fellowship-wide Services, 1986.

Baron, Renee, and Elizabeth Wagele. *The Enneagram Made Easy*. New York: HarperCollins, 1994.

Berne, Eric. *Games People Play*. New York: Ballantine, 1978.

Berry, Carmen Renee. *When Helping You Is Hurting Me*. New York: Harper and Row, 1988.

Bilodeau, Lorrainne. *The Anger Workbook*. Center City, Minn.: Hazelden, 1992.

Bradshaw, John. *Homecoming*. New York: Bantam, 1990.

Bramson, Robert. *Coping with Difficult People*. New York: Anchor Press/Doubleday, 1981.

Carnes, Patrick. *Out of the Shadows*. Center City, Minn.: Hazelden, 2001.

Carter, Jay. *Bipolar: An Unorthodox Approach*. Wyomissing, Pa.: Unicorn Press, 2001.

Carter, Jay. *Self-Analysis: A Kick-Butt Boot-Camp Approach*. Wyomissing, Pa.: Unicorn Press, 2001.

Dean, Melanie A. *Borderline Personality Disorder*. Salt Lake City: Compact Clinicals, July 1, 2001.

Dempsey, Mary H., and Rene Tihista. *Dear Job Stressed*. Palo Alto, Calif.: Davies-Black Publishing, 1996.

Ellis, A., and R. A. Harper. *A New Guide to Rational Living*. Englewood Cliffs, N.J.: Prentice Hall, 1975.

Ellis, A., and Raymond Tafrate. *How to Control Your Anger Before It Controls You*. New York: Citadel Press, 1997.

English, O. Spurgeon, and Gerald H. J. Pearson. *Emotional Problems of Living*. New York: Norton, 1963.

Gibran, Kahlil. *The Prophet*. New York: Alfred A. Knopf, 1923.

Gray, John. *Men Are from Mars, Women Are from Venus*. New York: HarperCollins, 1992.

Griffin, George. "The Case of the Costly Neurotic." Unpublished paper, 1983.

Hallowell, E. M., and J. Ratey. *Driven to Distraction*. New York: Touchstone, 1994.

Harding, M. Esther. *The Way of All Women*. New York: Harper & Row, 1975.

Hare, Robert D. *Without Conscience*. New York: The Guilford Press, 1993.

Hubbard, L. Ron. *Self-Analysis*. Los Angeles: The American Saint Hill Organization, 1950.

Jung, C. G. *Man and His Symbols*. New York: Doubleday and Co., 1964.

Keirsey, David. *Please Understand Me*. Del Mar, Calif.: Prometheus Book Company, 1998.

Klein, Allen. *The Healing Power of Humor*. New York: Putnam, 1989.

Lewis, C. S. *The Screwtape Letters*. New York: Macmillan, 1961.

Lombardo, Michael M., and Morgan W. McCall Jr. *Coping with an Intolerable Boss*. Greensboro, N.C.: Center for Creative Leadership, 1984.

McKay, Matthew, and Peter Rogers. *The Anger Control Workbook*. Oakland, Calif.: New Harbinger Publications, 2000.

Miller, Alice. *Banished Knowledge*. New York: Doubleday, 1990.

Mondimore, Francis Mark. *Bipolar Disorder*. Baltimore: Johns Hopkins Press, 1999.

Neff, LaVonne. *Mother Teresa*. Novato, Calif.: New World Library, 1989.

Norwood, Robin. *Women Who Love Too Much*. New York: Pocket Books, 1986.

O'Connell, David F. *Dual Disorders*. Binghamton, N.Y.: The Haworth Press, 1998.

Payne, Robert. *The Life and Death of Adolf Hitler*. New York: Praeger Publishers, 1973.

Peck, M. Scott. *The Road Less Traveled*. New York: Touchstone, 1978.

Prather, Hugh. *Notes on Love and Courage*. New York: Doubleday, 1977.

Rathus, S. A. *Essentials of Psychology*. Fort Worth, Tex.: Harcourt Brace, 1997.

Riso, Don Richard. *Understanding the Enneagram*. Boston: Houghton Mifflin, 1990.

Sheridan, John H. "Executives at the Breaking Point." Unpublished paper, Cleveland, Ohio, 1979.

Tannen, Deborah. *You Just Don't Understand*. New York: Ballantine, 1990.

Trachtenberg, Peter. *The Casanova Complex*. United Kingdom: Angus & Robertson Publishers, 1988.

Watts, A. *Ego*. Berkeley, Calif.: Celestial Arts Publishing, 1975.

Watts, A. *Time*. Berkeley, Calif.: Celestial Arts Publishing, 1975.

Wilde, Jerry. *The Anger Management Book*. East Troy, Wisc.: LGR Publishing, 1997.

Although I may not be able to answer all correspondence, I am interested in knowing how this book has affected your life. You may write me at the following address:

P.O. Box 6048

Wyomissing, PA 19610

Or you may contact me through my website:

jaycarter.net

You may also contact me regarding speaking engagements on:

- Gender issues
- Anger management
- Communication (still the number-one secret to success)
- Using the prefrontal lobe